Threats Pending
Fuses Burning

Threats Pending
Fuses Burning

Managing Workplace Violence

Dennis A. Davis

DAVIES-BLACK PUBLISHING
Palo Alto, California

Published by Davies-Black Publishing, an imprint of Consulting Psychologists Press, Inc., 3803 East Bayshore Road, Palo Alto, CA 94303; 1-800-624-1765.

Special discounts on bulk quantities of Davies-Black books are available to corporations, professional associations, and other organizations. For details, contact the Director of Book Sales at Davies-Black Publishing, an imprint of Consulting Psychologists Press, Inc., 3803 East Bayshore Road, Palo Alto, CA 94303; 415-691-9123; Fax 415-988-0673.

Davies-Black and colophon are registered trademarks of Consulting Psychologists Press, Inc.

Cover photography: Al Francekevich/The Stock Market

01 00 99 98 97   10 9 8 7 6 5 4 3 2 1
Printed in the United States of America

Library of Congress Cataloging-in-Publication Data
Davis, Dennis A.
    Threats pending, fuses burning : managing workplace violence / Dennis A. Davis.
       p.   cm.
    Includes bibliographical references and index
    ISBN 0-89106-102-9
    1. Violence in the workplace.   2. Violence in the workplace—Prevention.
I. Title.
HF5549.5.E43D388   1997
658.4'73—dc21   96–40266
                                             CIP

FIRST EDITION
First printing 1997

Contents

Preface

This book is about the growing problem of workplace violence. Most people would agree that violence in our society in general seems different now from what it was thirty years ago. Is there more violence in our society now? Or do we simply have better means of reporting it? Are people more willing to act out violently? Or have we always been this way?

These questions are debated by just about everyone at some point. Like everyone else, I have theories about why we see so much violence in our society, and more specifically, why we have violence at work. Before I share some of those theories, though, allow me to explain how and why I have developed my ideas.

For years now I have consulted to law enforcement agencies; some of them are local, some state, and some federal. I have come to admire and respect law enforcement agents. Not everyone is interested in taking on the responsibility of protecting the members of society. And not everyone who is interested is suited for the job. The men and women who are both interested and suited for the job are very special people. I have also come to loathe the agent of the law who is *not* suited for the job and who takes advantage of his or her position— using the badge or the baton, or the gun, to manipulate and harass others. I have spent a great deal of time helping organizations screen out such persons, developing and presenting new training sessions, and conducting critical incident debriefings.

In 1987, the two police sergeants with whom I had worked to develop training programs (Bill Nelson, now a lieutenant with his department, and Frank Bucheit, now retired) and I began to get calls from law enforcement agencies as well as from private companies. Many of these calls were from people inquiring about training programs. Many callers wanted to know if there were methods to detect who had the highest potential for violence, and if these methods could be taught. They also often wanted to know if there were methods to defuse individuals whose behavior had begun to escalate toward violence.

Some law enforcement agencies had long been teaching their employees how to detect an individual who was becoming a threat, and how to then defuse the situation before either the suspect or the officer got hurt. Bill, Frank, and I began to tailor the training sessions we had conducted with police agencies to fit situations in which non-police officers often found themselves at work. We found that many of the tactics that are used by good, successful police officers can be used by civilians as well. "Command presence," for example, simply describes how a person can send authoritative messages with his or her body, select words, and use tone. Similarly, keeping in touch with dispatchers and using the radio to communicate location are simply the specific ways that a police officer uses appropriate resources and support.

We began to think that if we shared this information with the civilian employee, he or she would be better able to resolve conflicts at work—and better prepared to deal with violent or potentially violent situations when they arose.

So began my attempt to understand workplace violence and thereby develop appropriate responses. More and more I was called on to train supervisors and managers in private companies. As the number of training sessions and speaking engagements increased, so too did the requests for a book on the topic. Many human resources professionals told me that they had thumbed through workplace violence books in the past but that they "all seemed like infomercials for the author." Other managers and supervisors reported that much of the reading in the field was interesting but focused primarily on the "war stories and not enough on understanding the people *behind* the war stories."

I have written this book in order to share my experiences as a consultant on preventing and responding to workplace violence. It is geared toward the practitioner/professional who seeks to understand what motivates some workers to violence and how and when to defuse potentially violent situations. I believe that the suggestions I offer in this book will help organizations protect people and property.

In this book I will describe violence generally, and violence in the workplace more specifically. Though I will use several extreme examples to drive home a point, I will seek to avoid many of the scare tactics—the blood and guts as well as the doom and gloom—often associated with books on this subject. There are two reasons for this: (1) Scare tactics don't work. Most often when people are frightened by something, their response is to look away in denial. (2) The most frequently occurring form of workplace violence is not the most extreme violence.

Instead I will seek in this book to help you to understand what motivates violent behavior, and to show you how to intervene before an extreme act occurs. While this is not a book about psychology per se, there are certain principles of psychology that are relevant to the study of violence. Psychology seeks to understand, predict, and influence human behavior. This book seeks to help the reader to understand violence—specifically, why certain individuals resort to aggressive means to accomplish an end result. Once you *understand* violence, there is a reasonable opportunity to *predict* who in an organization will become violent and under what circumstances. Then, and only then, can you *influence* the person's behavior so as to avoid tragedy.

I will not include the kinds of "war stories" so often found in books on this subject. Discussing war stories can sometimes lead to a greater understanding of the problem of workplace violence. Just as often, however, we get caught up in the sensationalism of the story and forget to find the lesson. The examples in this book are composites. They are incidents that have actually occurred that have been fictionalized for two reasons: (1) to protect the identities of individuals and companies, and (2) to refocus our attention away from "remembering that incident" and toward identifying those clues that might have helped identify the problem individual *before* the incident occurred.

Another significant way that this book will likely differ from others is the material in chapter 10, Assessing Your Organization's "Violence Quotient." Human resources, security, and personnel professionals have often asked for a way to assess their organization's strengths and weaknesses with respect to violence—both the potential for it and the response to it. Among consultants in this field, the tools for such an assessment have been well-guarded secrets. Now, however, in chapter 10 of this book, we provide detailed questionnaires that will allow you to assess your own workplaces. For it is one thing to have a consultant tell you the areas of concern within your company: You may or may not agree with the consultant's conclusions, and you may or may not do anything about them. But it is an altogether different experience to do your own assessment and uncover your own strengths and weaknesses yourself.

This book is organized into three sections: The Problem and the Perpetrators, Prevention and Intervention, and Case Studies and Assessment.

Section One, The Problem and the Perpetrators, provides an overview of workplace violence, complete with some important statistical information (chapter 1). It also defines the three stages of violent behavior (chapter 2), the common warning signs associated with future violent behavior in the workplace (chapter 3), and the typical profiles of potentially violent employees (chapter 4).

Section Two, Prevention and Intervention, is devoted to reducing the number of violent incidents at work through planning and preparation. It explains exactly what organizations need to do to establish a safe working environment, and includes sample policies to use as models when implementing a violence prevention program (chapter 5), as well as other tools for prevention (chapter 6). This section also places emphasis on recognizing the pattern of behavior associated with increased risk for violence, as well as on early intervention. It describes principles of intervention and analyzes specific dangerous situations (chapter 7).

Section Three, Case Studies and Assessment, starts by offering you a chance to learn from others' mistakes (chapter 8) as well as benefit from what organizations are doing right to decrease their risk and liability (chapter 9). We then provide several self-tests (chapter 10) that are designed to help you become aware of your company's strengths and weaknesses.

Finally, appendix A summarizes the major steps your organization will need to take to start a workplace violence prevention and intervention program; and appendix B lists resources nationwide offering violence prevention services.

Whether you choose to institute a workplace violence prevention and intervention program on your own or seek outside assistance in doing so, be sure that you do *something* to protect your company's employees and assets. More than that, make sure that violence prevention and awareness become an integral part of your organization's culture. Hold meetings, distribute memos, and post notices on bulletin boards on the topic of preventing and responding to workplace violence. If you have a company newsletter, include a regular column of updates on your company's program and advice on detecting and reporting any warning signs of violent behavior. If you have an employee of the month or similar awards program, incorporate violence prevention and awareness as factors to be considered (or give special awards for accomplishments in those areas). Develop questions on violence prevention and response procedures to use on tests and in interviews for promotions. Perhaps distribute phone cards reminding all employees of what numbers to call in case of an emergency, what steps to take if they observe (or are the victims of) violent behavior, and what the reporting procedures are. In short, make certain that you reinforce for all employees, as often as you can and in as many ways as you can, that your company will not tolerate violent behavior—and that the security and safety of the people who work there are its highest priorities. We believe taking these steps can help you minimize the threat of violence in your organization.

A Note on Profanity

The use of profanity and other foul and offensive language often goes hand in hand with violent behavior. This is not to say that everyone who ever curses or utters an ethnic slur is going to commit an act of physical violence. However, almost all of those persons who do commit acts of violence use profanity and other offensive language—before, during, and after the act—to describe or discuss both the victim and the violence itself. Think of soldiers at war, two drunken men getting into a brawl, or a man beating up his wife or girlfriend: It would be more unlikely if these perpetrators *didn't* use curse words, slurs, and other foul and offensive language.

There are a number of reasons for this association between violent acts and the use of offensive language. People who commit acts of violence tend to be very angry, and foul language is one common way in which such anger manifests or expresses itself. Also, as we discuss further in chapter 2, except when fighting in self-defense, most humans need to objectify and dehumanize others before they can commit acts of violence against them. The use of curses, ethnic slurs, and other degrading verbal imagery is both an expression of this objectification and one means of achieving it. Finally, words can be weapons: We can hit and hurt each other with demeaning names and offensive statements just as we can hit and hurt each other with fists and rocks and guns and knives. And, in fact, given that violent behavior is a *process* that often escalates in intensity (again, see our discussion of the three stages of violent behavior in chapter 2), hitting someone with words is often a preliminary step on the way to hitting someone with fists or other more powerful weapons.

We would be remiss, therefore, and untrue to the real nature of violent behavior, if we omitted all profanity, slurs, and other foul and offensive language from the examples and case studies we refer to throughout this book. We have tried to refrain from quoting most of the more obscene and incendiary words and phrases that those who commit violent acts can, and often do, speak. However, please be forewarned that we have not watered down the language of violence in this book completely. Our purpose in using select (as opposed to gratuitous) profanity and other foul language in some of our examples is not to offend our readers—and if we do, we most certainly apologize for it— but rather to more effectively communicate the anger and volatility of the potentially violent person.

The Author and the Publisher

The Problem and the Perpetrators

This section is devoted to uncovering the scope and impact of workplace violence. We will review recent statistics, which demonstrate that the incidence of violence at work is on the rise. We will also clearly define violence and the three stages of escalation toward violent behavior. Finally, we will describe the warning signs of potential violence and give some typical profiles of violent individuals.

Is Workplace Violence a Real Issue?

According to widely accepted statistics, workplace violence has a major impact on businesses in the United States. In 1992 there were over 111,000 incidents of workplace violence. And this number accounts only for reported incidents. It has been suggested that 43 percent of those who are threatened and 24 percent of those who are attacked at work don't even report the incident. Workplace homicide has been described as the fastest-growing category of homicide in the country. The U.S. Department of Labor's Bureau of Labor Statistics reported in the 1995 National Census of Fatal Occupational Injuries that there were 1,004 homicides at work in 1992, 1,063 in 1993, and 1,075 in 1994. Homicide is the second leading cause of death on the job for men. And as if that isn't alarming enough, homicide is the leading cause of death on the job for women.

It is estimated that corporate America spends $4.2 to $6.4 billion per year in the aftermath of workplace violence. That money is spent on many different things, including increased security and protective measures, relocation and/or repair of existing property, increased absenteeism, increased attrition rates, trauma care for employees (for both physical and emotional trauma), stress disability retirements, and loss of productivity due to employees' needs to share and compare experiences with others on the job. Yet, as of 1994, an estimated 80 percent of American companies and organizations had not taken any steps toward dealing with the prospect of aggression and violence at work. Of the companies that have done anything at all, 97 percent have done so in reaction to a particular incident. Much of this underreaction is due to the belief that violence is "random and unpredictable." If one accepts this premise, then the natural conclusion is, "So why bother spending the energy or the money if it can still happen anyway?"

Out of the Blue

A man walks into an office building and sprays an office with gunfire. Several people get wounded. Perhaps someone dies. Later that evening, the media go into that man's community and speak to his neighbors. "What type of neighbor was Mr. Y?" The most common description? "He has always been the nicest guy in the world—always willing to lend a hand. Who could have guessed that he'd do something like this? He must have just freaked out."

The above interchange might take place hundreds of times each year. But it is a myth! Human behavior is not organized in such a way that a "perfectly normal," hardworking family man wakes up one day and suddenly decides to act out his rage in a manner that leads to the injury or death of others. There are always warning signs. There is always a pattern of behavior or at least an individual behavior that warranted a closer look.

> The most common description of a person who perpetrates violence is, "He was the nicest guy." However, this is not true. There are always warning signs.

How, then, to explain why there is always someone in the vicinity who describes the violent behavior as occurring "out of the blue"? The answer is denial or ignorance. Imagine the scenario described above, only this time the neighbor being interviewed says, "You know, Mr. Y was always strange. He did spiteful little things, and I knew it was only a matter of time before someone would get hurt." What would the very next question be? "Why didn't you *do* something or *tell* someone?" Realizing that you had vital information but failed to act appropriately can lead to tremendous guilt when something tragic happens. A very natural response (usually unconscious) is to deny one's early perceptions to avoid such feelings of guilt.

There are of course times when neighbors, family members, and co-workers are truly ignorant of the significance of certain behaviors. These individuals readily acknowledge that they noticed certain "inappropriate" behaviors on the part of the perpetrator, but simply did not give these behaviors the urgent attention they required. A similar explanation is that these people just weren't thinking. Something might be obvious in retrospect, but we might not be able to see it or know it at the time. Try the following simple exercise to experience this phenomenon:

> There are ten words for human body parts that all have three letters. These are all proper terms, not vulgar or slang. They are all easy to spell, and we learn them all when we are children. How many can you name? Give yourself a two-minute limit. The answers are on the bottom of the next page.

If you're like most people, you were probably able to name six or seven of these commonly known body parts. Yet you probably recognized them all right away when you turned the page and saw them listed.

Guilt and ignorance are two major factors influencing our false perception that violence is random or unpredictable. However, workplace violence is neither random nor unpredictable.

As you read through the descriptions of workplace violence that follow in this book, remember the above exercise. Just as the three-letter body parts are as obvious as the nose on your face, so too are the signs that there is or may be a problem. You will see that human behavior in almost every area, at almost every stage, is made up of *processes*, not *events*. Typically humans do not flip-flop from one state to another. Rather, most of the changes we go through—including behaviors escalating toward violence—are process-oriented, and that means change over time.

Answers: arm, ear, eye, gum, hip, jaw, leg, lip, rib, toe

2

The Three Stages of Violent Behavior

The process of becoming violent is just that—a process. It does not happen overnight. Nor does the individual one day simply "flip out." Rather, there is an increase over time in inappropriate behavior: an increase in the frequency of the acting out, an increase in the intensity of the acting out, and an increase in the threat level of the behavior.

As you are about to see, we have broken down this process of becoming violent into three separate and distinct stages: early potential, escalated potential, and realized potential. These three stages are developmental. In other words, as an individual moves through them, he or she is moving closer to actual physical violence.

Stage 1: Early Potential

When one examines stage 1 violence, there is a tendency to minimize the behaviors as "inappropriate" perhaps but not necessarily violent. After all, the individual displaying the behaviors listed in the accompanying box on page 11 hasn't put his or her hands on anyone, or even threatened to put his or her hands on anyone. How, then, might one reasonably say that these behaviors are acts of violence?

Objectification and Dehumanization

There are certain inhibitions that prevent most people from hurting others physically. In fact, most humans will inflict pain and/or suffering on others in one of only two situations. The first is for self-defense. Given the right (or the wrong) circumstances, most of us will fight to our deaths to protect ourselves or our loved ones. Fortunately, most of us will rarely if ever find ourselves in a situation in which we have to fight for our lives.

However, the second common situation in which we allow ourselves to hurt others is when we have first objectified and/or dehumanized another person. *Objectification* and *dehumanization* are two words that describe the act (usually unconscious) of rendering a person less than human—and therefore less than ourselves. Once I see a person as less than human, the social inhibition that makes harming another person difficult no longer has any influence. We can't see what others are thinking, but thoughts are often portrayed in words. Consider the following two examples:

1. During times of war, every nation dehumanizes its enemies. Soldiers can be heard referring to their enemies as "dogs," "beasts," and other derogatory terms. This is because it is difficult to shoot, bomb, and otherwise maim

Characteristic Stage 1 Behaviors

The following behaviors are characteristic of stage 1, indicating *early potential* for violence:

- Objectifying and dehumanizing others
- Challenging authority
- Regularly becoming argumentative
- Alienating customers or clients
- Originating and spreading lies about others
- Swearing excessively; using sexually explicit language
- Abusing others verbally; sexually harassing others

and kill other human beings. However, a dog is not a human; it's acceptable, even desirable, to kill a beast.

2. A woman is walking from her car to her home. A man comes up behind her and yells, "Give me your purse, bitch!" The question that comes to mind is, if he's going to rob her, why does he have to add insult to injury by insulting her as well? The answer, of course, is that in the event that the woman decides *not* to hand over her purse, the robber will have to hit her or otherwise use force to get it away from her, and in order to do that, he cannot see her as a mother, sister, or daughter, because he has women like that in his life, and presumably feels some sympathy toward them. Instead, he has to see her as a nonperson. (Another answer might be that the abusive language is a preliminary expression of violent behavior, and that he's using it in an attempt to control her actions—by the implied threat of more advanced, nonverbal expressions of violence. In this case, he's *already* hitting her—with words—and has had to dehumanize her in order to do so.)

How do these two scenarios relate to work? If there is some-one in the work setting who, on a regular basis, refers to others by things other than their names, that person is exhibiting stage 1 violent behavior. If there is someone at work who is argumentative and refuses to cooperate, that person is exhibit-ing stage 1 violent behavior. If there is someone in the office who puts others down and verbally abuses them, that person is exhibiting stage 1 violent behavior. Most often, of course, peo-ple behaving in these ways don't realize that their behavior is in fact a form of violence. But it is—and it needs to be dealt with accordingly.

Do Not Minimize This Behavior

Overwhelmingly, stage 1 violent behavior accounts for the majority of workplace violence. In addition to being difficult to deal with, these people pose serious problems for the organiza-tions in which they work. For, make no mistake about it, this behavior creates a hostile work environment for others. And sexual harassment is another type of behavior that leads to a hostile work environment. Sexual harassment can take many forms: making sexually explicit jokes, discussing one's private sexual fantasies and exploits, and pursuing a fellow employee (whether romantically or sexually) who does not want to be pursued. We hope that by now it is clear to managers and other administrators that there is a major liability for the company whenever a hostile work environment exists.

Slurs Are Never Only Words

A question often asked is, "Why do we make such a big deal over racial or ethnic slurs? After all, such slang terms are only words." The answer is that they are *never* only words. There are two primary reasons to disallow this type of expression in pro-fessional settings:

1. When an individual refers to others by these types of derogatory terms on a regular basis, it isn't long before it is possible for that individual to stop viewing certain groups as human.

2. Even if the speaker of these epithets doesn't become physically violent, often the recipient of such harsh language has been socialized to respond in a violent manner. It is all too common for one employee to toss out a racial slur, and then to feign innocence and victimization when the recipient lashes out in response. For the manager or administrator, sorting out who is at fault (probably both of them) can be a nightmare. It is more important to make sure that such incidents never happen to begin with.

> Dehumanization and objectification are the first signs that an individual has moved toward violence. Remember, violence starts with thoughts and moves first to language then to actions.

Stage 2: Escalated Potential

Stage 2 is the "bridge" stage. Individuals exhibiting stage 1 violence generally don't commit acts of violence, but individuals exhibiting stage 2 behavior are very close to doing so. They are still considered "potentially" violent, but are closer to realizing that potential. Take a minute to look at the behaviors listed in the box on the following page, then let's examine why stage 2 violent behavior is so menacing.

Blatantly Disregarding Organizational Policies and Procedures

In any bureaucratic organization, most of the members of that organization believe at some point that those at the top have

Characteristic Stage 2 Behaviors

The following behaviors are characteristic of stage 2, indicating *escalated potential* for violence:

- Arguing frequently and intensely
- Blatantly disregarding organizational policies and procedures
- Setting traps for others
- Stealing from the company or from other employees
- Making verbal threats
- Conveying unwanted sexual attention or violent intentions by letter, voice mail, or e-mail
- Holding others responsible (blaming others) for all problems or difficulties

no idea what's really going on. However, if the organization in question is the company we work for, in consideration of our need to make a living most of us will not act out. After all, who can afford to be jobless? But some people lose sight of that basic consideration, or disregard it, and cross over a line into inappropriate behavior.

Review the following discussion, then see if you can determine the attitude being displayed by the employee.

Manager: Fred, I'm coming to you because I'm worried about your recent actions. I really have to insist that you get approval from purchasing before you go out and spend six thousand dollars on a new computer. You could get us both in trouble.

Employee: Look, I know what I need to buy. I don't need to fill out any stupid paperwork.

Manager: Yes, I know that you know what you *think* you need, Fred, but it might not be part of the company's plans for right now. You could be suspended.

Employee: Whatever!

Manager: But, Fred, you've been suspended twice already this quarter for spending without approval. You know the company's policy on this—three suspensions in the same quarter leads to an automatic termination. Is that what you want to happen?

Employee: You do what you've gotta do!

Manager: It's a hard job market out there, Fred. How will you survive?

Employee: I'm not worried about that.

In the above exchange, the employee is displaying one of the scariest attitudes a potentially violent person can have. It is the same attitude or perspective that makes a terrorist so frightening: that of *not caring*. Most people will occasionally gripe about bureaucratic requirements or changes at work—a new report that has to be written, a different manufacturing technique, or some additional mandatory training. However, when all is said and done, most employees do what they are required to do. When an individual outright refuses to comply, that person is telling the world that he or she doesn't care—not even about him- or herself. "I don't care if I get fired. I don't care if I can't feed my family. I don't care what you think of me."

If a person doesn't care about him- or herself, how much can that person care about other workers in the environment? The answer is, Not at all. What's the connection to violence? Imagine a terrorist for whom it is important to go home at night, have dinner with the family, and tuck the kids into bed. How scary would this terrorist be? Not very. In fact, what makes terrorists so frightening is the

> Society is governed by order and structure, which is often conveyed by rules. Be concerned with those people who totally disregard the rules. They are demonstrating a classic *don't care* attitude.

attitude they typically display: "If I die, then I die. My life isn't that big a deal. The cause I'm fighting for is more important than my life, than your life—than anyone's life."

Stealing from the Company or from Other Employees

The kind of stealing we're referring to here is *not* the stealing of valuable goods and merchandise necessarily. At least the stealing of valuable objects makes sense. The perpetrator can perhaps sell them and make a few dollars. What we're referring to here is the stealing of small, insignificant things—"stupid" things, some might say.

Why would an individual steal a carton of staples? How useful can a 300-count box of rubber bands be? These items aren't stolen for their value. Instead, the individual who commits such thefts acts out of an attempt to express frustration and anger, and to get revenge. He or she is trying to "stick it" to the company. Many managers and administrators pay little or no attention to such "petty" thefts on the part of their own employees. In fact, in many retail industries employee theft is seen as "part of doing business." However, we contend that this behavior must be seen as violent acting out.

Imagine being so angry that you just have to do something to hurt someone. So you decide to steal some useless items from work—some office supplies, perhaps. In a rational state of mind, you understand that this act won't bring any real satisfaction. However, in an irrational state you might expect to feel fulfilled by this act. What might happen if, after stealing the item, you found that you had no real use for it and that no one in the office even noticed it missing? The probability is that you would be further frustrated by gaining no satisfaction from your risky act. And you might even be angered that the item wasn't missed. The next time you decide to act out, you'll need to do so in an angrier, more noticeable manner. The danger of employee theft, therefore, is the risk of escalation of angry behavior by the perpetrators.

Making Verbal Threats

There's a line of thinking about verbal threats that goes something like this: "People who act just act. People who threaten really just want attention. The best thing to do is ignore them." However, this may be one of the most ridiculous theories in the world. For there are certain things that rational people simply never form their mouths to say. When was the last time someone you know to be rational shouted, "The next person who asks me for anything better be prepared to meet his maker!"? Rational people do not make comments like this. Sure, we all fantasize about hurting someone who really makes us angry. But basic etiquette and a desire to conform to social norms restrain most of us from verbalizing these threatening thoughts. A person who does verbalize such thoughts, even in jest, is out of control or fast approaching the point of being out of control.

> All threats of violence must be taken seriously, just as airport security must take all threats about bombs and hijacking seriously.

Conveying Unwanted Sexual Attention or Violent Intentions by Letter, Voice Mail, or E-Mail

Let's start with the person (let's assume it's a man, though it could be a woman as well) who sends a note to a co-worker detailing his sexual interest. Assuming that such interest or attention is unwanted and unreciprocated, this is, of course, sexual harassment. But our concern here goes deeper than just the company's liability in these matters. We saw in our discussion of stage 1 behaviors that the person who presents a threat for violence also often presents a threat for sexual harassment. Think back to the last time you had to investigate an alleged incident of sexual harassment. One of the things you probably noticed was that the harasser carried out his acts in a subtle, maybe even sneaky manner. Perhaps the words used were ambiguous, making it hard to know his real intent. Perhaps the harasser made certain that there were no other persons nearby to overhear his inappropriate comments. In many cases, the victim doesn't even report the incident. And even when the incident is reported, it is often the word of the victim against the word of the harasser. Depending on the harasser's status and reputation in the organization, he just might get away with it.

Now, entering stage 2 violent behavior, the harasser has taken to writing down his inappropriate comments, or recording them on voice mail, or sending them in e-mail messages. The concern here is that such actions demonstrate a lapse in judgment. Is there anyone left in the American workforce who *doesn't* know that sexual harassment is illegal? Probably not. Is there anyone who doesn't know that an investigation would soon identify the originator of the offending e-mail? Again, probably not. The odds are clearly stacked against the perpetrator. Why, then, would the perpetrator take such a risk and commit to paper or hard drive such blatant breeches of policy? Most likely because, in his slipping logic, he has failed to consider the consequences of his acts. And the danger here, beyond the sexual harassment itself, is that most people who ultimately act out violently do not consider the consequences of their behavior either.

Holding Others Responsible (Blaming Others) for All Problems or Difficulties

The combination of blaming others and making verbal threats should cause the most concern of all stage 2 behaviors. Here we

> Making verbal threats and the tendency to blame others often constitute a lethal combination.

are not referring to the occasional situation most people have experienced in which they are truly the victims of another's negligence or malice. Rather, we are talking about the person who takes *no* responsibility for any problem situation in which he or she may find him- or herself. Consider the following discussion:

Manager: Tim, you have been late three out of the last four working days. Not only that, but each day you have been at least forty-five minutes late. We are trying to run a business here, and cannot tolerate this. Is there something I can do to help you with this problem?

Employee: No, it's just my stupid wife!

Manager: Excuse me?

Employee: Yeah, she doesn't wake me up on time.

This exchange could very well be dismissed as a sign of immaturity on the part of the employee. However, it must be given second consideration. People who blame others tend to see things as "me against the world." Their perspective often includes the idea that they are being picked on (a persecution complex). They tend to perceive themselves as being pushed into something out of their control. Often they perceive the world as unfair only to them, and can't understand why others seem to mistreat them.

People who feel picked on, or at least believe that they have been pushed, eventually back into a wall or corner. Often when they perceive that they have been backed into a corner, they will come lashing out—believing that anything they do is justified by the fact that they have regularly been mistreated. While we are not focusing on extreme incidents of violence in this book, be assured that in most documented cases, the perpetrator has held others at least partly responsible for his or her predicament and actions.

Stage 3: Realized Potential

While stages 1 and 2 describe a progression in the potential for physical acts of violence, stage 3 describes the realization of that potential. See the accompanying box on page 21 for some specific examples of stage 3 violent behavior.

Getting Involved in Physical Confrontations and Altercations

There is a tendency in our society to minimize fistfights as "no big deal," especially if the two participants are men. It's easy to view this behavior as "just the guys mixing it up." However, this is a gross underestimation of the significance of this behavior.

Between the ages of eight and ten years old, little girls develop the skills to resolve conflicts verbally as opposed to physically. They learn to talk it out. Young boys are generally slower in their development of such skills. However, by the age of eleven to thirteen, they too have usually learned to talk issues out and resolve conflicts with words as opposed to fists. That is not to say that there are never occasions when boys and girls who have passed the above-mentioned ages get into physical fights. However, such occasions should become more and more rare as they reach and pass those ages.

If there are men and/or women in your place of business who allow themselves to get into pushing and shoving matches, take punches at one another, or invite others to fight them, these people have two major problems. First, they haven't developed appropriate mechanisms for defusing their anger and tension. People such as these often become so overwhelmed with their own anger or frustration that they lose control. And once out of

Characteristic Stage 3 Behaviors

The following behaviors are characteristic of stage 3, indicating *realized potential* for violence (for example, actual violence):

■ Getting involved in physical confrontations and altercations

■ Displaying weapons (guns, knives, pepper spray, etc.)

■ Committing or attempting to commit assault, sexual assault, arson, or suicide

control, there are few if any limits to their acts of rage. Think of someone you know who is quick to resort to physical challenges. Such people often believe that their rage will overpower the individual they see as the cause of that emotion. They rarely consider the possibility that they might be overcome by their opponent. In fact, they are usually too "wound up" to consider the prospect of losing the altercation. In many cases when the person with the quick temper is "bested" in a fight, this only means that he or she will have to escalate to the next level of aggression. And that next level often involves weapons.

The second problem of people who are so willing to fight (other than in self-defense) is that they don't care about their own physical safety and survival. Their behavior is tantamount to saying, "I'm so mad that I don't care if I get hurt." Remember that if a person doesn't care about his or her own physical safety, he or she can't possibly care about anyone else's. And it's the attitude of not caring that makes that person so dangerous.

> There is no such thing as "a little pushing and shoving." Adults don't get into fistfights, except if they are defending themselves or their loved ones or are out of control.

Displaying Weapons

People who flash weapons generally have reached the point of being ready and willing to use them. In a sense, they've already "gone too far." By the time an employee or customer flashes a gun or other weapon, that person has already violated the policy of the company and has likely broken the law as well. At best, he or she will lose his or her job or, in the case of a customer, certainly will not be welcomed back to the business. At worst, the police will be called and either the person with the weapon will be arrested or a shoot-out will ensue. Given that these are the choices, what do you suppose the person with the weapon has to lose? In his or her mind, probably not much.

Attempting Suicide

Suicide in our society is very often a last-resort act of desperation. And desperate people are dangerous—both to themselves and to others. There is a correlation between suicide and depression. One of the most common indications that an individual may be suicidal is his or her lack of energy coupled with deep despair. Other signs that a person may be contemplating suicide include the lack of planning for the future. Most people plan ahead in their lives: imagining what they will do with their tax refund, deciding what to wear to a Halloween party, or planning future vacations. Often the suicidal person doesn't make these kinds of plans because he or she can't imagine being around for these events. Other indications that a person may not plan to be around much longer include giving away prized possessions, putting one's financial and business affairs in order, and completing tasks that have remained undone for a long time.

There is also a correlation between depression and anger. In fact, it is understood that suicide is a very angry act. While not all suicidal people are angry, sometimes anger is the predominant emotion. This anger can be expressed through loud, angry outbursts, in bitter discussions about death and dying, and by engaging in activities that have a high accident rate. The angry suicidal person is most threatening, both to him- or herself and to others, when the anger is coupled with talk about weapons and methods of dying. The danger here, again, is that the individual is displaying a lack of concern for his or her own safety. And if a person isn't concerned with his or her own safety, the safety of others is certainly in question as well.

Commonly Asked Questions

Very often people will remark that they know someone who exhibits some of the behaviors we have just described and classified, but certainly don't believe that that person is violent. This leads to some commonly asked questions, which we will address here.

Does everyone exhibiting stage 1 behavior go on to become a serial killer?

No. In fact, the percentage of individuals who go on to perpetrate major acts of violence is relatively small. However, in the overwhelming majority of cases of extreme violence, the perpetrator demonstrated one or more of the stage 1 behaviors on a regular basis beforehand.

How would you differentiate those whose behaviors are escalating toward violence from those who just have some really bad habits?

Probably you couldn't. Which is why it is important to notice all of the behaviors early on.

Does every individual who acts out in an extreme manner go through all three stages?

Yes—even if the escalation isn't readily apparent to some. The fact is that human behavior is not *event*-oriented but rather *process*-oriented. Consider what we commonly refer to as puberty. When we talk about it, we generally refer to it as an event. In actuality, though, it is a period or process of change that begins much earlier than is commonly believed. Or consider the supposed phenomenon of "overnight success" in the world of arts and entertainment. It's a myth! No one becomes a success overnight, at anything. If you talk to the movie star or pop singer or novelist who's suddenly getting a lot of attention from the media and buying public, you'll invariably find that that person has been practicing his or her craft—performing in unheard-of venues, taking classes, writing things that no one ever read—for years, often for decades. This is how people really develop artistic talent: gradually, over a long period of time. So it is with violence: It doesn't just appear overnight.

How long does one's behavior remain in each stage before escalating to the next level?

The time it takes for any one individual's behavior to escalate from stage 1 to stage 3 varies. There is no single answer for all people, and it would be dangerous to try to suggest one. Suppose you were told that each stage lasted for about three weeks. When you first encountered someone in stage 2, would you intervene immediately? Or would you think that you had some time to delay before responding?

How many of the various behaviors at each stage does one need to identify in order to confirm that there is a problem?

The answer is twofold. First, one sign is all that is required to identify a problem. Let's say that Mary is observed dehumanizing her coworkers by the way she speaks to and about them. We could say that Mary is exhibiting stage 1 violent behavior. Part two of this answer is that you will rarely if ever see only one behavior. We hope our discussion has made it clear that the person most likely to become violent is usually the person causing trouble in many areas in the organization. In the above example, if Mary is swearing at coworkers or using inappropriate language to describe her office mates, she has demonstrated her potential for violence in several ways: She is objectifying people; she has created a hostile work environment that might cause the company legal concerns; and, assuming the company has policies prohibiting such language, she has also failed to obey company policy. Thus, we can see that observing a single inappropriate behavior is extremely unlikely.

Is this behavior categorization applicable only in work settings?

Absolutely not. While we like to believe that we are totally different in different settings, the fact is that human behavior is pretty consistent across the board. That is to say that while we may dress a little better for work, and maybe we relax our language somewhat around friends, we are who we are at work, at play, and at home. Imagine an elementary school–aged child who is having some problems at home. He isn't responding to his parents' demands and refuses to do his homework. He also gets into fights with other children in his neighborhood. What is the probability that this child is behaving appropriately at school? Very slim. This child is likely to refuse the teachers' commands and probably gets into fights with the other kids on the playground as well. So it is with the individual who demonstrates potential (if not actual) violence at work: The likelihood that this person is behaving in a similar manner at home is great.

> Look around you. The people who are violent at work are the same people who are violent at home, on the road, and in the grocery store.

Why does a person's behavior escalate from stage 1 to stage 2 and then on to stage 3?

There are many reasons that explain why escalation occurs. The first, and probably the most disconcerting, is that the individual is out of control. Remember, exhibiting the stage 1 and stage 2 behaviors we have described doesn't guarantee that a person will move on to actual physical violence. These behaviors do, however, provide an indication of the individual's *propensity* for violence. In other words, people who have acted out in the past have demonstrated some of the behaviors in each of the three stages. Out-of-control and desperate people behave in out-of-control and desperate ways. A person whose violent behavior escalates can be said to be "losing control" over time. Also, many of the people who behave this way are experiencing considerable frustration, which is a feeling of being powerless and unable to influence one's own situation. The person who screams, for instance, believes he or she is not being heard otherwise. Sometimes escalation occurs because the individual believes that increased violence (or manipulation or whatever) is the only way to be heard.

Violent behavior can also escalate because of increased tolerance on the part of those observing it. An example of this can be seen with television. Remember when a love scene consisted of two adults walking into the bedroom and staring lovingly into each other's eyes, then the program cut to a new scene or to a commercial? Today, of course, all but the most explicit details are shown right there on TV. Or remember during the Gulf War when a national political leader said on national TV, "Saddam, we are going to kick your ass!"? As we become more comfortable—or more accurately, *less uncomfortable*—with such depictions or instances of sex or coarse language or violence in our lives, we allow more and more of what would normally be seen as inappropriate language or behavior. Our tolerance for it increases. When Tim swears at his boss, and the boss as well as other administrators ignore the behavior, the message to Tim is that his behavior was not out of line. Over time, this has the effect of increasing all employees' tolerance for such behavior.

Do the three stages of violent behavior include all those behaviors that are known to correlate to violence?

No. There are other behaviors and characteristics that have high correlations to violence but do not fit neatly into our three stages (for example, there is a .84 correlation between substance abuse and violence). However, because these other behaviors and characteristics can be observed in all three stages of violent behavior, we have designated them "Warning Signs" and will discuss them in detail in the next chapter.

chapter 3

The Warning Signs of Violent Behavior

There are nine danger signals, or warning signs, associated with an increased risk for acting out; these are listed in the accompanying box on page 30. As we review each danger signal, we will discuss its underlying meaning and why it is associated with violence. These behaviors and characteristics do not exclusively belong in stage 1, 2, or 3. Rather, they can be observed in any of the three stages. These behaviors and characteristics *always* warrant a closer look and rarely surface alone. More often than not, they occur in conjunction with other warning signs and/or stage 1, 2, or 3 behaviors.

These nine danger signals are highly correlated to workplace violence. A question we are often asked is, "How many of these warning signs do I need to see to conclude that there might be a problem?" The answer is, Only one. For these behaviors are

The Nine Warning Signs of Violent Behavior

1. Fascination with weapons

2. Substance abuse

3. Severe stress

4. Violent history

5. Severe changes in psychological functioning

6. Decreased or inconsistent productivity

7. Social isolation and poor peer relationships

8. Poor personal hygiene

9. Drastic changes in personality

not one-time occurrences. Rather, they are almost always part of a pattern, and are usually suggestive of an overall style of non-compliance.

Fascination with Weapons

It is important here to differentiate "fascination with weapons" from mere "ownership of weapons." People who own weapons are rarely violent. Often the friends and co-workers of a person who owns weapons don't even know that he or she has them. They're rarely discussed, unless the subject somehow comes up in conversation, and when the subject does come up, the person who owns weapons talks about them in a matter-of-fact way.

Gun ownership is *not* the same as fascination with guns. Mere ownership is not a cause for concern; fascination is.

The individual who is *fascinated* by weapons, on the other hand, wants everyone to know that he or she has them. Such people tend to talk about their weapons at every opportunity. In fact, they are often uninterested in discussing anything else. When frustrated or angry, such a person might make such comments as these: "I know how to get justice," or "I'll bet a bullet would help get my point across." While it sounds incredible that someone would actually make such comments, there have been several widely publicized incidents wherein a perpetrator of violence had previously told everyone around him of his weapons collection and his frustration with others. In one case, someone who went on to commit severe acts of violence had actually said beforehand, "My nine millimeter does all my talking for me."

The underlying message here is, "I don't feel confident enough in my ability to get my point across without my weapon." In addition, such a person is often saying, "I don't feel that I'm heard or taken seriously unless I mention that I have a gun."

Think of Robert DeNiro in the movie *Taxi Driver.* In that movie he played a character who drove a taxi in New York, who felt insecure and inadequate. He did not relate well to others and often responded in a defensive or paranoid way to the big, bad city around him. He had poor posture, he mumbled when he spoke, and he displayed little that could be identified as confidence. Yet there's a wonderful scene (wonderful in terms of illustrating a point) in which he's in his apartment, standing in front of a mirror. He now has a gun hidden on his body, and he's practicing being confident. We observe a visible metamorphosis. His posture is now erect, with his chest out and his head held high. His words are clear and well projected. "You talkin' to

Table 1 Warning Sign #1		
Fascination with Weapons		
Stage	**Violent Behavior**	**Example**
1. Early potential	Objectifying others	Ted tells a co-worker, "Those idiots upstairs, they don't understand anything I've been trying to tell them. I bet they understand a thirty-eight special."
2. Escalated potential	Making verbal threats	After his supervisor has asked him twice to do something he doesn't want to do, Ted says, "I heard what you said. Ask me to do it again, and I'll introduce you to my friend Smitty Snub-nose."
3. Realized potential	Displaying weapons	Later that same day, he stands in the door to his supervisor's office and pulls back his jacket to reveal a gun in his waistband.

me?" he says. "You must be, 'cause I don't see anybody else. Yeah, I think you must be talkin' to me." Just then he reaches into his waistband and practices quickly drawing his gun.

This classic scene illustrates the "fascinated" person's belief that a gun or other weapon is the great equalizer. Such a person likes to make it known that he or she possesses weapons, knows how to use them, and believes that there is no better way to be understood.

Table 1 continues this example of how fascination with weapons might manifest itself in an escalating progression of violent behaviors.

Substance Abuse

First, let's understand that drugs and alcohol don't *cause* an individual to act out. More accurately, they *allow* a person to act out. People who act out violently have possessed the potential to do so all along. When one isn't drinking and/or indulging in other mind-altering substances, it's easier to conform to social norms, which means it is more likely that one will do and say only those things that are appropriate for the setting. However, with the introduction of alcohol and other drugs, there is a tendency to disregard social norms. According to Joseph Kinney, in National Safe Workplace Institute's 1996 *Workplace Violence and Aggression Risk Reduction Training Manual,* there is a .84 correlation between violence and substance abuse, which means that 84 percent of documented incidents of workplace violence occurred at the hands of individuals who were either chronic substance abusers or under the influence at the time of their act.

To further understand the connection between substance abuse and violence, consider the following example.

Ed and Rudy have each worked for the same manufacturing company for about ten years. About eighteen months ago, they both applied for the same promotion. Ed, while perhaps somewhat better qualified, knew in advance that the job would probably go to Rudy. Ed reached this conclusion when he observed Rudy and the company's vice president having lunch and overheard them discussing what Rudy planned to do with the additional money he would be making from the raise. When the announcement was made three weeks later that Rudy would be moving into management, Ed, though disappointed, made plans to attend the promotion party and congratulate Rudy. Ed knew this was the smartest thing to do because another promotion would be made in six months, and he wanted to show everyone that he was a patient team player. However, alcohol was served at the party, and Ed decided to have a few drinks before approaching Rudy. By the time Ed made his way over to shake Rudy's hand, he had had four drinks. As he approached Rudy, he overheard some other managers discussing what a wise choice Rudy was for the promotion. Just then Ed chimed in, "He was only a good choice because he's been such a brown-noser for the last two years."

Ed's behavior in this situation provides a simple example of how alcohol and other drugs can lessen one's reasoning abilities and allow one to act on impulse rather than thought. Rationally, Ed understood what the right behavior was (to congratulate Rudy graciously). However, under the influence of several drinks, his reason gave way to his true emotions and he behaved inappropriately (by insulting him instead). Moreover, chronic substance users/abusers don't necessarily need to be actively under the influence for their behavior to be violent or otherwise inappropriate. Rather, regular use/abuse over time can corrode their judgment and lower their inhibitions permanently. Think of someone you know who has a drinking problem, who regularly says and does the most outlandish things. We don't generally think that such people are at risk for violence—until they do something violent—but they are.

> Substance abuse is a major factor in the overwhelming majority of documented incidents of workplace violence.

Table 2 continues this example of how substance abuse might manifest itself in an escalating progression of violent behaviors.

Severe Stress

In many ways severe stress is similar to substance abuse: It does not *cause* one to be violent. It can, however, *allow* one to be violent. What we are referring to here are major life events that occur all at once or rapidly on top of each other.

Table 2	Warning Sign #2	
Substance Abuse		
Stage	**Violent Behavior**	**Example**
1. Early potential	Objectifying others	At the office party celebrating Rudy's recent promotion, Ed says "He was only a good choice because he's been such a brown-noser the last two years."
2. Escalated potential	Making verbal threats	A little later, Ed and Rudy find themselves alone in the men's room together. "Come on, Mister Butt Kisser," Ed says, holding his fists in a boxer's pose, "let's see if you've got any guts. I'll knock your lights out."
3. Realized potential	Committing assault	Rudy tries to defuse the situation by taking Ed's comment and pose as a joke, but when he makes a few mock head feints in response, Ed punches him in the face.

Marge has recently been disciplined at work for her frequent tardiness. She explains that she has been coming in late because her 3-year-old son has a severe illness and has been hospitalized for the last month. In addition, Marge recently found out that her husband was having an affair, and she demanded that he leave the house. This, of course, has left her to deal with her sick child on her own. Yesterday, Marge received a notice from her insurance carrier that she would no longer be covered under the medical plan because of an inconsistency in her application. And finally, because she is now solely responsible for the mortgage, Marge has been late with her payments the last four months and completely missed two payments. The bank has notified her that it is beginning foreclosure proceedings.

Stress doesn't kill. But stressed-out people some-times do.

Given the combination of major stressors described, would anyone be surprised if Marge became depressed and suicidal? Probably not. Now let's suppose that a male co-worker, who has always found Marge attractive, learns of her recent separation and, not knowing the other difficult circumstances she's facing, starts flirting with her and pressuring her to go out with him despite her protestations that she's not interested. This final stressor could be the proverbial straw that breaks the camel's back. Marge could get very angry at her pursuer; she could yell at him, she could scream profanities, she could strike him or threaten to kill him if he doesn't stop hitting on her. And although most people can sympathize with Marge's frustration and anger in this situation (some might even say that the male co-worker got what he deserved), the point is that Marge must be considered at high risk for violence because of the combination of major life stressors weighing down on her at this time.

Table 3 continues this example of how severe stress might manifest itself in an escalating progression of violent behaviors.

Violent History

One of the best predictors of future behavior is past behavior. If an individual has demonstrated violent behavior (as described by any of our stages) in the past, there is a greater probability that such behavior will surface again. When people have learned how to use manipulation and bullying to get what they want, there's no reason for them to spontaneously abandon such tactics, particularly if they have been successful for them. In fact, a tendency toward bullying, manipulating, and badgering often develops early in life and becomes a lifelong pattern.

Table 3	Warning Sign #3	
Severe Stress		
Stage	**Violent Behavior**	**Example**
1. Early potential	Objectifying others	Marge, whose young child is in the hospital, tells a co-worker of her difficulties getting her insurance carrier to pay for some necessary procedures. "Insurance administrators, my husband, my boss—they're all men," she says, "and they're all assholes."
2. Escalated potential	Making verbal threats	A few days later, Marge says, "My son and everyone else would probably be better off without me around, so maybe I won't be too much longer."
3. Realized potential	Attempting suicide	That night, she swallows her entire prescription of Valium pills.

An offshoot of this type of behavior that must not be overlooked is domestic violence. Whenever there is domestic violence, there is the risk of workplace violence. This applies whether the employee is the victim or the perpetrator. Why the perpetrator poses a threat at work is easy to understand: This is a person (usually a man) who uses violence to control people and situations in order to meet his needs. As we have already seen, there is no reason to assume that a person who uses violence in one area of life (personal) will not resort to violence in other areas of life (professional) as well. In fact, the opposite is true: We tend to behave in similar ways in different circumstances.

> Ignoring the fact that a co-worker is involved in an abusive relationship helps no one. Not the co-worker, not ourselves, not the company.

Why the *victim* of domestic violence poses a severe threat to her work environment is not generally acknowledged. However, the scenario in which a co-worker (generally a woman) is the victim of domestic abuse is often *more* threatening than having a perpetrator of domestic violence in your office. Consider the following example.

> Joyce has been married to Dan for ten years. She has worked as a dental assistant in the same office for the last eleven. While she and Dan were dating, she regularly came to work in tears, and occasionally she had bruises and cuts that she described as having resulted from falls. Over the last four years, her co-workers have noticed that her "falls" have become more and more frequent, and the injuries sustained in them have become increasingly severe. Finally, she confesses to a close friend at work that she has been battered all these years and would like help in getting away from Dan. Her co-worker gives her the name and number of a women's shelter. Joyce contacts the shelter and moves there one day while Dan is at work. Fearing for her safety, she leaves no forwarding address or phone number. She simply leaves Dan a note saying that she is okay and asking him to not try to find her.

> Many people don't like the implication, but a prior history of violence is the best predictor of future violence.

In the above scenario, there is still one place where Dan assumes he can find his wife— at work during her normal working hours. And he'd probably be correct in making this assumption. We don't usually give up our jobs when we flee

Table 4	Warning Sign #4	

Violent History

Stage	Violent Behavior	Example
1. Early potential	Objectifying others	Dan phones his wife, Joyce, who has just left him, at her office. "You ungrateful bitch," he says, "after all I have done for you, you pack up without warning."
2. Escalated potential	Making verbal threats	Joyce tries to tell him that she gave him plenty of time to change his abusive ways toward her. Realizing his hold on her has diminished, Dan says, "You'd better be home tonight, or you're really gonna regret it."
3. Realized potential	Getting involved in physical altercations	The next day, Dan shows up at Joyce's office. When one of Joyce's co-workers tries to block Dan's entry, Dan shoves her out of the way and lunges at his wife.

an abusive partner. If and when Dan shows up to confront Joyce, she and everyone else in her office building will be at risk. (Even if she left her job in order to avoid him, he is still likely to show up at her office. When he is told that Joyce is no longer employed there, do you think he will believe this and leave peacefully? Not likely.)

Table 4 continues this example of how a violent history might manifest itself in an escalating progression of violent behaviors.

Severe Changes in Psychological Functioning

The Americans with Disabilities Act (ADA) states that everyone has the right to earn a living, even those with mental and/or psychological disabilities. It also requires that employers make "reasonable accommodations" for those with challenges. These requirements are appropriate and reasonable. Despite myths to the contrary, people with psychological disorders are overwhelmingly *not* violent. Moreover, the small percentage of that population who are violent are not likely to hold down steady jobs, and therefore don't generally pose threats to the workplace. There are, however, certain circumstances affecting this population that are associated with a deterioration in mental functioning, and that therefore can present a threat of violence. One of these circumstances is when an individual who is under the supervision of a doctor and on medication stops taking the medication. There could be many reasons for doing so; however, the two most common are "changes at home" and "feeling better."

To understand what we mean by "changes at home," you need to understand a few things about people with severe mental and/or psychological disorders. Generally such people are unmarried, live with one or more relatives, and are not completely independent. They can usually go to work on a regular basis and perform their jobs with a moderate to high level of functioning. They like and need structure, so they're good at following instructions. However, change is both confusing and threatening to them; they're more comfortable with routine. At work they may be perceived as a little "different" but generally harmless.

Such individuals tend to operate best "in the here and now." They're generally not good at planning for the future or foreseeing consequences. This is where the relative or relatives at home come into play: They help the psychologically challenged person to function. The following might be a typical exchange:

Debbie: Mike, how many pills do you have left?

Mike: Let's see . . . one, two, three, four, five, six. I have six.

Debbie: Okay, I'd better call the doctor and get that prescription refilled before you run out. You're still taking them every day, right?

Mike: Right. I take them with my cereal in the morning.

The point of this exchange is that Mike can't figure out for himself that if he doesn't get his prescription refilled he's going to run out soon. He needs someone else to do that for him—in this case, his sister, Debbie.

Now let's suppose that there are changes at home. Debbie's going to get married. She's distracted by all the planning and decision making that that requires, and she forgets to check if Mike's prescription is close to running out. Or worse, she forgets to check that he's even taking his medication every day. So Mike runs out of pills—and doesn't say anything. Or he just stops taking them even though he still has some left. What happens then? The answer is that Mike's functioning can begin to deteriorate (though gradually; like other behavioral changes, this is a process, not an event). Such deterioration might be evidenced by such signs as the following:

- Having conversations with individuals not seen by others
- Talking about personal adventures too fantastic to be real
- Work habits (timeliness, completeness, reliability, etc.) changing drastically
- Showing signs of irritability and/or argumentativeness

To understand what we mean by "feeling better," you have to understand the effects of psychotropic medications. If they work as they're supposed to, they give the person the feeling that he or she is well (and therefore, perhaps, no longer *needs* the medication). At the same time, they're likely to have unpleasant side effects—which give the person taking them even more reason to want to stop. You may know someone who has stopped taking his or her high blood pressure medication, for example, for similar reasons. So you can understand how a person with disordered mental functioning might choose to discontinue taking his or her psychotropic medication.

Let's return to Mike in our example above. But let's suppose now that he lives alone and that his level of functioning and independence are such that his doctors don't think he needs a caretaker. Recently he was promoted at work, from mailroom clerk I to mailroom clerk II. And lately he's been socializing regularly with a new friend he met at the gym, where he likes to exercise in the evenings. Given this combination of "things going right" in his life, he might well decide that his doctors are idiots who don't know what they're talking about, and that he doesn't really need his medication. Should he stop taking it, though, his co-workers are likely to notice subtle changes in his behavior and functioning over time.

"Changes at home" and "feeling better" describe two different scenarios in which a person with serious psychological disorders stops taking his or her medication—which could potentially lead to violent or otherwise inappropriate behaviors. Another circumstance that's similarly risky is when the person continues to take his or her prescribed medication but it's no longer effective in controlling the disorder. Such a diminishment or loss of effectiveness could be caused by many things: weight loss or gain, hormonal changes, interactions with other medications, and/or an incorrect dosage.

In all of these circumstances, the key factor you want to be on the lookout for is a drastic or severe change in psychological functioning. Such changes will probably occur gradually, however. If Mike forgets to take his medication Monday morning,

Table 5 Warning Sign #5

Severe Changes in Psychological Functioning

Stage	Violent Behavior	Example
1. Early potential	Alienating customers	Mike, who works in the mail room, responds to voices only he can hear. "You damn Martians better get out of here!" he shouts at visitors he doesn't recognize.
2. Escalated potential	Making verbal threats	He begins to perceive his co-workers as part of a conspiracy that's out to torment him. "I know you want to possess me," he tells a fellow employee one day, "but I'll kill you before I let you take over my soul."
3. Realized potential	Attempting assault with a deadly weapon	Mike begins carrying a baseball bat with him at all times. He says it's to ward off the Martians, but he swings it at anyone who gets near enough to touch him.

he's probably not going to act out Monday afternoon. But if he *stops* taking his medication Monday morning, his demeanor is likely to change over the ensuing weeks.

The other thing to remember is that although people with serious psychological disorders can become violent, it is rare that they do so. And when they do, it is usually not with an intent to harm, but rather the result of being out of touch with reality.

Table 5 explores this example of how this warning sign—

> Our assumptions about how people with serious psychological disorders act are usually inaccurate. Those who can hold down a job are usually not violent.

severe changes in psychological functioning in those with serious psychological disorders—might manifest itself in an escalating progression of violent behaviors.

Decreased or Inconsistent Productivity

Most people adopt work habits that stay with them for a life-
time. People with high quality standards, or those who take
pride in their work, generally maintain certain high standards
over their entire careers.
Therefore, when there is a
decline in a person's productivity, or when a person's productivity is so inconsistent as to be
unpredictable, this can be a
sign of problems. The biggest
concern is that the individual

> There is always something more to decreased or inconsistent productivity than what is immediately apparent.

has moved into an "I don't care" mode. As we saw earlier, the
attitude of not caring can carry over into many areas and thus
poses a potential threat. There are many other possible explanations for changes in productivity, all of which warrant a closer look.

- The person could be angry or frustrated about some real or
  imagined slight, and could be actively attempting to sabotage
  the company or individuals within the company.

- The person could have developed a substance abuse problem,
  and his or her productivity could be directly related to the
  use or nonuse of chemical substances.

- The person could be under severe stress for reasons unrelated to work, and the productivity decline or inconsistency
  could be the result of a periodic inability to focus on his or
  her job.

Table 6	Warning Sign #6	
Decreased or Inconsistent Productivity		
Stage	**Violent Behavior**	**Example**
1. Early potential	Challenging authority	Charlie has missed several important deadlines over the past few weeks—which is very unlike him. When his manager tries to discuss this with him, Charlie says, "Don't you realize I don't give a damn about this company? Why don't you get out of my face."
2. Escalated potential	Making verbal threats	The next day, Charlie refuses to apologize for what he has said. "What are you gonna do about it?" he says to his manager. "I'll wipe the floor with you or anyone else who tries to make my life difficult."
3. Realized potential	Attempting suicide	A little later, Charlie admits that he is despondent over the recent death of his young daughter and the subsequent breakup of his marriage. His manager recommends that he take some time off and seek treatment for depression. But that night, Charlie tries to kill himself by running the engine of his car in a closed garage.

Each of these possible explanations for the change in productivity can pose a threat for violence—which makes identification of the reason for the change essential.

Table 6 presents an example of how decreased or inconsistent productivity might manifest itself in an escalating progression of violent behaviors.

Social Isolation and Poor Peer Relationships

The second most common description of the individual who perpetrates severe violence (after "nice guy," which isn't true) is "loner." This description typically is accurate. Loners can be divided into two different subgroups: the avoided and the avoiders. The "avoided" refers to the person whom most people in the organization will avoid at all costs. People often describe this person as "spooky," "strange," or "weird." And their efforts to avoid this person can be extreme. In one organization, the man who was the most knowledgeable about the workings of computers was also so disagreeable that his peers reported spending hours (on their weekends, without pay) trying to figure out certain programs just to avoid dealing with him.

The "avoider," on the other hand, refers to the person who will attempt to avoid others at all costs. Very often, this individual sees him- or herself as somehow better or smarter than everyone else. Such persons often describe their peers as "idiots" and other derogatory terms, and describe any attempt to relate to others as "a waste of time and energy." One manager in a utilities company described a case in which an employee quit rather than work with a partner, which the company's safety regulations required.

Both avoiders and the avoided are associated with increased risk for violence. Why? Because humans are social beings. We need contact with other humans in order to thrive and stay healthy emotionally. Consider that most of us have developed interpersonal support networks in our lives. When things aren't going smoothly, we plug into our network to help cope with stress. Sometimes we use our friends and loved ones to vent our frustrations, or to find a compassionate ear. Sometimes we just want a good belly laugh or a little distraction—a few hours at a friend's house to forget what troubles us. And sometimes our interactions with others help remind us that things aren't quite as bad as we thought they were. After all, *everyone* has occa-

> We choose to be alone sometimes, but we don't choose to be loners. This is what results when we have alienated the people around us.

sional (or constant) difficulties in life: Focusing on someone else's problems for a change can take us away from our own.

The problem with the person at work who has alienated everyone in the office is that he or she has likely done the same at home. Remember, contrary to what most of us believe, we are not significantly different from one place in our lives to the next. What does the person who has alienated both everyone in his or her professional life and everyone in his or her personal life do to cope with stress? To whom does this person turn for sympathy and support? Maybe no one. And, sadly, the lack of supportive relationships can lead to feelings of frustration, anger, depression, and hostility. Left unchecked, these feelings can lead to homicidal and suicidal behaviors.

Table 7 gives an example of how social isolation might manifest itself in an escalating progression of violent behaviors.

Poor Personal Hygiene

Have you ever been around a person whose body odor was so offensive that you couldn't tolerate being around him or her for more than a few minutes? Or have you ever known a person who was normally well groomed and neatly attired, who suddenly started showing up at work looking as if he or she had

> A "bad hair day" is one thing. A "bad hair (breath, clothes, body odor, etc.) week" is altogether different.

slept in his or her clothes? It's unlikely that these people are unaware of the reactions others are having toward them. The more probable explanation for this behavior is that the person just doesn't care.

Table 7 Warning Sign #7

Social Isolation and Poor Peer Relationships

Stage	Violent Behavior	Example
1. Early potential	Objectifying others	Whenever Mary, who is a loner, is assigned to work on a project with another person, she finds something to complain about. "Everyone knows those people are stupid," she says about her new partner, who happens to be a person of color.
2. Escalated potential	Setting traps for others; stealing	Mary attempts to sabotage her new partner, Diane, by deleting some important files from Diane's computer.
3. Realized potential	Committing arson	But the plan doesn't work; Diane has backup files that Mary didn't know about. So Mary, in her frustration, does something even more extreme: She drops a lit match into the wastebasket underneath Diane's desk.

It takes a lot of time, patience, and attention to detail to present ourselves in a professional manner each day. Very often the first sign that a person has moved into an "I don't care" mode is his or her lack of attention to personal hygiene. And when an individual stops caring about him- or herself, it is difficult (if not impossible) for that person to care about others. Having concern for others forces us to imagine what it feels like to be in their shoes (empathy). With empathy, it is difficult to hurt another person. Without empathy, it is far easier to inflict pain and suffering.

When a person stops caring about him- or herself, this may be a sign that his or her capacity for empathic feelings has diminished as well. This can spell trouble for those of us who share space with the noncaring person.

Table 8 gives an example of how poor personal hygiene might manifest itself in an escalating progression of violent behaviors.

Drastic Changes in Personality

Most of our personality characteristics are fairly stable. We can and do change our behaviors according to where we are, our mood, and other variables. But who we are generally stays with us for life. The third most common description of the individual who perpetrates severe violence (after "nice guy," and "loner") is "the quiet

> The quiet person may simply be shy or modest and therefore shouldn't necessarily cause us concern.

type." You may have heard someone say, "You'd better be careful of the quiet person, because under all that surface calm is a volcano waiting to erupt." The fact is, however, that being the quiet sort is no more related to being violent than being the loudmouth. Often the person who is not extremely talkative is simply more shy and modest than other people in the office. What *should* cause us concern, though, is when there is a sudden and drastic change in the way a person expresses him- or herself.

> The loudmouth may be annoying and hard to take for long periods of time, but he or she is not necessarily violent.

When the formerly quiet individual begins to express an opinion about everything, this may be a sign that the person has felt picked on in the past

Table 8　Warning Sign #8

Poor Personal Hygiene

Stage	Violent Behavior	Example
1. Early potential	Abusing others verbally	Eric has recently started showing up late for work, wearing clothes that are disheveled and dirty. When a colleague jokingly asks if Eric's washing machine is broken, he tells the person to go to hell.
2. Escalated potential	Making verbal threats	Eric's work, like his personal appearance, becomes sloppy and unreliable. He sends a long e-mail memo to the company president detailing everything that's wrong with the organization. "If you think I'm going to continue to put up with this shit," he concludes, "you've got another thing coming to you."
3. Realized potential	Getting involved in physical altercations	Normally clean-shaven and neat in his appearance, Eric now has a scraggly beard and is in need of a haircut as well as a shower. One morning when Eric shows up for work, a security guard who has just started working for the company asks Eric what business he has there and refuses to let him pass through the lobby. Eric goes ballistic: Refusing to show his I.D., he berates the security guard and tries to force his way into the building. He even gets into a shoving match with the security guard before someone recognizes him and intervenes.

and has decided to stand up for him- or herself. The thought process reflected in this sudden change may be something like this: "You people have been pushing me around for the entire ten years I've been here, and I'm not going to take it anymore." The person experiencing this reaction may consider it to be self-defense. Remember, though, that self-defense is one of two situations in which we allow ourselves to inflict pain and suffering on another person.

Table 9 gives an example of how this warning sign—drastic changes in personality—might manifest itself in an escalating progression of violent behaviors.

In the next chapter, we will discuss several profiles of potentially violent employees. These profiles are directly connected to the nine warning signs discussed in this chapter. Moreover, we will continue to explore how these warning signs might manifest themselves in an escalating progression of violent behaviors.

Table 9 Warning Sign #9

Drastic Changes in Personality

Stage	Violent Behavior	Example
1. Early potential	Sexually harassing others	Rob is normally courteous and mild-mannered around the office, but lately he has been making rude and inappropriate comments about his assistant, Leslie, focusing on her clothes, lipstick, and various parts of her body. Usually he makes these comments to other (male) employees, but in such a way that Leslie overhears them.
2. Escalated potential	Conveying unwanted sexual attention	He has left some ambiguous but certainly inappropriate notes on her desk. One said, "Leslie, please come into my office as soon as you return. I have some urgent needs requiring your attention." Leslie has tried to maintain a professional attitude toward him; but he's been asking her out to lunch almost every day, and complaining loudly about the torment she's causing him by refusing. One day he leaves her a scribbled note begging her to give him one chance to please her in bed. He assures her she will not be disappointed.
3. Realized potential	Committing sexual assault	Rob asks Leslie to work late one afternoon, and when their floor is mostly deserted, he calls her into his office, closes the door, and tries to force himself on her physically.

chapter 1

Typical Profiles of Potentially Violent Employees

In this chapter we will identify and describe certain profiles that are associated with a high incidence of violence. See the accompanying box on page 54 for a list of the nine typical profiles, which correspond directly to the nine warning signs described in chapter 3. You will notice, however, that the individuals described in each profile often display more than one of the nine warning signs. Also, they often exhibit behaviors that can be classified in more than one of the three stages of violent behavior described in chapter 2. In the case of an individual displaying multiple warning signs, the thing to remember is that the more warning signs of potential violence you observe, the more likely it is that that person will become violent. And in the case of a person exhibiting behaviors that span two or more of the stages of violent behavior, the thing to remember is that you must

Nine Profiles of Potentially Violent Employees

1. The gun fanatic
2. The substance abuser
3. The employee facing severe stress
4. The person with a violent history
5. The employee with severe changes in psychological functioning
6. The employee demonstrating decreased or inconsistent productivity
7. The socially isolated employee demonstrating poor peer relationships
8. The employee demonstrating poor personal hygiene
9. The employee demonstrating drastic changes in personality

categorize the person at the *highest* stage of violent behavior he or she exhibits—which we will do at the end of each profile.

Profile 1
The Gun Fanatic

Virgil is a 42-year-old warehouse worker for a large manufacturing company. He started working for this company eight months ago after responding to a classified ad in the newspaper. His employment history is sketchy at best, though he claims to have worked for many years on an oil rig. (The company did not confirm his work history before hiring him.) Virgil takes pride in being able to take care of himself. He often speaks about the lack of justice in contemporary society, and claims that he would not call the police if he ever found himself in an emergency. When asked by co-workers what he would do if someone was breaking into his house in the middle of the night, he responds without hesitation that he would "take a life in a heartbeat." Furthermore, he seems to relish the prospect of doing so.

Virgil's one obsession seems to be his gun collection. He drives far out of his way to attend gun shows on his days off, he seems to go to the local shooting range several nights each week, and he's always talking about the new guns he's just bought or would like to buy. Virgil, who doesn't have a wife or girlfriend, seems to spend almost all his free time, energy, and money on this hobby. Indeed, at times he talks about his guns as if he is sexually attracted to them, or gets a sexual thrill somehow from having and using them. He calls them by pet names, all female, and he sometimes says things like, "Yes, sir, Nina sure is a pretty little thing." ("Nina" is his 9 mm semiautomatic.)

On one occasion a fellow worker made the mistake of joking that it sounded as if Virgil was in love with his guns. The other workers who heard this remark nodded their heads and laughed. Virgil waited for their laughter to die down, then said to the man who had cracked the joke, "You think you're real funny, don't you? Maybe someday me and my guns'll just have to teach you a little lesson in respect—then you'll see just how in love we really are." Virgil's tone and statement scared all the men who heard him that day. The man who'd made the joke quickly apologized to Virgil, saying it was a stupid thing for him to say and that he just hadn't been thinking. Virgil said, "You're damn right about that." Then the man left the area as soon as he could.

On another occasion, while in the lunch room, Virgil overheard some workers discussing gun control—specifically, a proposal to place a national ban on the sale of automatic weapons (or those that could easily be converted to automatics). Virgil, who hadn't really been part of the conversation and seemed to have missed the gist of it, angrily said, "If anybody ever tries to take away my guns, there'll be a bloodbath." Everyone fell silent. One woman, who didn't know Virgil that well, said, "That's a little extreme, don't you think?" Virgil said "No" and glared at her. Witnesses describing the scene afterward said that he looked as if he wanted to rip her head off. Eventually he turned and stormed out of the room.

After these two incidents, Virgil's co-workers began to retreat from any interaction with him. All he ever seemed to want to talk about was his guns, and there always seemed to be an edge of hostility in his tone. (Virgil was mad at the entire world.) Some of his co-workers started reporting to their supervisor that they were afraid of Virgil and didn't want to have to work with him. A few even indicated that they thought Virgil carried a gun at work; they hadn't actually seen one, but he'd made a few comments to suggest this, and it seemed to fit with his overall obsession and character.

Virgil presents the classic signs of a person who is obsessed with weapons—in his case, guns. He's insecure and a loner; he probably feels powerless in most areas of his life. But his guns give him a sense of authority and control. He wants everyone to know that he has this authority and power, so he has to tell everyone about his guns all the time. This is his way of getting people to respect him. He exhibits a number of stage 1 violent behaviors (objectifying others, regularly becoming argumentative, and swearing excessively). But it would be most accurate to classify him as exhibiting stage 2 violent behavior (arguing frequently and intensely, and making verbal threats). And if he is actually carrying a gun at work, then he's very close to stage 3 (displaying a weapon). In any case, his potential for further violence should be considered extremely high.

Profile 2
The Substance Abuser

Steve is the 29-year-old vice president in charge of programming for a small but growing software company. He and a friend from college started the company during their senior year. After two years, the company went public, and it now has nearly eighty employees, tens of millions of dollars in annual revenues, and a major share of the market for its specialized products. Steve is not as flashy and personable as his partner, who is the marketing whiz of the pair, but is generally considered to be both the technical and the operational brains of the organization. Without him, the company would have no products and little direction.

Steve has acquired two nicknames during his seven-year career with this company: Boy Wonder and Boozer. "Boy Wonder" because of his youthful appearance, because he seems to be successful at anything he attempts to do, and also because he doesn't seem to need sleep the way normal adults do. Steve is famous for spending thirty-six or even forty-eight hours straight at the office. He's never missed a deadline he's set for himself, or failed to deliver on a project. Most of the employees admire him for his apparently tireless work ethic: He sets the standard that they all try to match.

"Boozer," however, refers to the dark side of Steve's work habits. When he stays up working around the clock for several days at a time, he gets so wired from adrenaline and sleep deprivation that he periodically takes a "taste" of alcohol to help him relax. For a while he kept a bottle of Russian vodka in the freezer in the kitchen on his floor, so some of his colleagues were well aware of when he was drinking and how much. Lately he's switched to rare aged scotches, which he keeps in his own office, so it's a little harder for others to monitor his drinking at work. But occasionally they smell it on him, and he has a tendency to become impatient and somewhat intolerant of others' mistakes and limitations after he's been drinking, so most of his colleagues can still tell when he's been drinking from this indirect evidence.

No one has ever questioned Steve's drinking at work—not officially, anyway. He was one of the founders of the company, and in many ways is the driving force behind it still. He works ridiculously long hours—and actually gets a lot accomplished, too—and if he feels he needs a few drinks to do so, why should anyone think there's anything wrong with that? (That's the common rationalization, anyway.) What his colleagues have done is develop a system for warning each other. If Steve has stayed up all night but is sober and approachable, they refer to him as "Boy Wonder." But on the mornings after he has stayed up all night and has been drinking, they refer to him as "Boozer" as a signal to avoid crossing paths with him.

One day Steve's administrative assistant, Darlene, arrived early and began her normal routine of turning on the lights and copy machines, opening blinds, and generally preparing the office for the business day. Not noticing that Steve was in his office, she went in there to open the blinds. He was lying on the floor behind his desk, either sleeping or trying very hard to rest after having stayed up all night. Raising the blinds made a fair amount of noise and flooded the room with bright sunlight. Suddenly Steve jumped up from the floor—which startled Darlene considerably. "Jesus Christ, can't you see I'm trying to sleep?" he shouted at her, and as he did so, he picked up a stapler from his desk and threw it at her, barely missing her head. Darlene was too shocked to speak or move. "Go on, get the hell out of here," Steve said. "What do I have to do, throw something else?" With that, she fled the office, making sure to close the door behind her.

About an hour later, Steve emerged from his office. Looking disheveled and somewhat embarrassed, he apologized to Darlene with the feeble excuse that he'd "had a rough night." He then said he was going home for a while, and left.

That afternoon he returned, having showered and shaved and put on clean clothes. He smiled at Darlene as if nothing was amiss, and told someone else that he'd had a great nap and felt ready to work all night again.

Steve has a drinking problem—period. He shows several of the classic signs of alcohol abuse: personality changes and increased aggression when under the influence, and a neglect of other needs such as food and sleep. Remember that there is a .84 correlation between workplace violence and substance abuse. In addition, it's probably safe to say that Steve is operating under a lot of stress, which poses an added risk factor. Given that he threw a stapler at his assistant and almost hit her in the head, we'd have to classify him as exhibiting stage 3 violent behavior (attempted assault). He didn't just threaten to throw a stapler (which would be stage 2 violence); he actually threw it.

Furthermore, it would be wrong to minimize his behavior by saying that he's "only" aggressive or verbally abusive after he's been drinking. For he drinks regularly at the office, and it is precisely the unpredictable nature of substance abuse that poses a major threat. What if he'd hit Darlene with the stapler? What if she hadn't been standing as far away from him as she was when he threw it? What if he'd picked up an empty scotch bottle and smashed it over her head? Then Darlene would likely be in a hospital—and Steve would likely be in jail.

Profile 3

The Employee Facing Severe Stress

Helen is a 43-year-old customer service representative for a catalog sales company. She's been with the company for five years, and has always been considered stable and steady. She has always described herself as having "the perfect life and the perfect family." However, she recently separated from her husband of twenty-two years (David) after discovering that he had been molesting their 13-year-old daughter (Sara) since she was six. Helen and Sara are currently living at a women's shelter while the local social services agency investigates the child molestation charges that Helen has brought against David.

Because of Sara's understandable need to be in regular contact with her mother, she has been calling Helen at work many times a day for the past several weeks. Helen tries to be attentive to her daughter's needs (she has, after all, been traumatized by the abuse and must now deal with the breakup of her family and the loss of her home as well), but these calls have definitely interfered with Helen's productivity and ability to focus on her work.

Moreover, Helen has begun to question herself out loud in such a way that it seems clear these events are constantly on her mind. Co-workers have repeatedly heard her ask herself, "How could I have let this go on for so long? How could I have not known?" Not only does she feel guilty and responsible for what has happened to her daughter, but, to make matters worse, the social services agency is investigating her as well, to try to determine if she knew of the abuse and didn't do anything about it. They say this is standard practice in such cases, but Helen is nonetheless terrified at the prospect that her daughter may be taken away from her and put into a foster home or state-run care facility of some kind.

David does not know where Helen and Sara are staying; he does not even know the phone number. And Sara started going to a different school when she and her mother moved to the shelter. So the only place David knows of where he can reach either of them these days is Helen's office. For a couple of weeks now, he's been calling her there repeatedly. At first he denied that he had ever touched Sara inappropriately. Then, when Helen refused to speak with him further, he acknowledged that some inappropriate incidents might have occurred, but if they had, he blamed Helen and her lack of interest in sex for driving him to seek solace elsewhere. (The disparity between Helen's low sex drive and David's seemingly insatiable one has always been a source of conflict in their marriage, and this comment only makes Helen feel more guilty and responsible for the abuse her daughter has suffered.)

David has begged Helen not to cooperate with the investigation, and to make their family whole again. He has promised to see a therapist to deal with his problems. However, he has also threatened Helen, saying that if she doesn't drop the charges against him, he'll say that she did it too—or at least that she knew about the abuse and didn't do anything to stop it—to ensure that Sara will be taken away from both of them.

As the investigation proceeds and the case against him builds, David is becoming more and more angry at his wife and daughter— and his threats are becoming more aggressive in both tone and substance. The other day, he told Helen, "You'd better stop all this lying and come home right now. Don't make me come down there [meaning, to her office] and do something we'll all regret." At which point Helen, who had never been seen to lose control before, screamed into the phone, "Don't you dare come near me, or I'll kill you, I swear I will." She then slammed the phone down and had to leave her desk for several minutes before she was calm enough to resume work.

Helen is clearly, and understandably, overwhelmed by the circumstances in which she finds herself. Prior to her discovery of what her husband was doing to her daughter, she considered her marriage a happy one, her life and her family perfect. Now, not only has she lost all of that, but she's living a daily nightmare—and feels guilty and responsible for what her daughter has suffered as well. She's living in a strange place, receiving threats from her husband on an almost daily basis, and facing the risk of losing custody of her daughter. Without a doubt, she's facing severe stress in her life, for a variety of reasons and in a variety of ways.

It should come as no surprise to anyone that her productivity at work is being affected by her current situation. In addition, however, we must note that she herself has exhibited stage 2 violent behavior (making verbal threats). Looking at her entire family situation, however, we'd have to say that because of her husband, David, this employee poses a stage 3 threat of violence. David has not only threatened her (stage 2), he has also (allegedly) committed sexual assault, an example of stage 3 violence. And the more desperate his situation becomes, the greater is his hostility toward his wife and daughter—who, in his eyes, are responsible for all the trouble he now finds himself in. Cases such as this one have the potential to escalate quite dramatically, with the husband stalking, battering, and possibly even attempting to murder the wife who has left him for a shelter and is bringing charges against him. And the likely scene of these possible future acts of violence will be Helen's place of work.

Some might argue that it is unfair to consider Helen a potentially violent employee, that she's the victim in this situation and shouldn't be blamed for her husband's misdeeds and volatility. The point to emphasize, though, is not that Helen herself is a potentially violent employee, but rather, that the overall circumstances of her present situation pose a grave risk for further violence.

Profile 4
The Person with a Violent History

John is a 52-year-old former banker. He is a large man, about six feet, two inches tall and now extremely overweight, though he was leaner and more athletic when he was younger. He is married and has two adult children. He's also very frustrated in his career. He used to be a mid-level manager in the mortgage department of a major bank, earning almost a six-figure salary. However, a couple of years ago, he was laid off as part of a cost-cutting measure. For a while he worked as a "consultant" to the banking industry, but his assignments were few and far between, and what he really wanted was a high-paying job with full benefits—and all the security that goes along with that.

Several months ago, John took a job as the manager of a small consulting firm. His salary is about half of what it was before he got laid off, and although the firm has a lot of potential, he considers his position beneath him. But he wasn't offered any of the banking positions he applied for, and he felt he needed to take this job to bolster both his flagging self-esteem and his dwindling bank account. His new company is made up of young and middle-aged professionals who are bright and headstrong. Though opinionated, they respect each other's views and know how to hash out their differences in a fair and courteous manner. Unfortunately for John, almost all of them know more about the consulting business, and their particular market and clients, than he does, which causes him to feel flustered and frustrated more often than he'd like.

John is used to using his size to get his way. In both his personal and his professional life, he's long been in the habit of intimidating others by literally standing up to them (in most cases, towering over them), pointing his finger at them (sometimes actually poking them in the chest), and speaking very forcefully (some would say yelling) until they submit to his wishes or his side of an argument. In his old position at the bank, he tended to hire young women with limited education and experience as his underlings and assistants because he found it was easy to get them to follow his directives without asking questions or otherwise challenging him. On the rare occasion when a colleague would challenge him, he used his size, his age, and his masculine bravado to browbeat him or her into submission.

In his current position, however, the professionals on his staff challenge him on a regular basis. Not only that, but his intimidation tactics rarely cause them to back down. Most of these colleagues are men themselves, so they're not intimidated by him because of that. And although he's older and bigger than they are, they're fit and smart and they know it, so they don't back down from anyone (especially not when they're right, which they usually are in their conflicts with John). The problem is that John cannot accept not being lord of this little fiefdom. Lately his yelling has been more frequent, louder, and more intense. (And some of his colleagues have responded by yelling back at him.) John has also taken to slamming doors and abruptly hanging up on people to end conversations that aren't going his way. The members of the firm who are White (as John is), have frequently heard him use racial slurs to describe other colleagues and client contact persons who are not. And he has on several occasions suggested that he might have to take a particular nemesis on a "hunting trip" on which "an unfortunate accident" just might occur. It is difficult to tell whether these comments are joking or serious—indeed, they seem a strange combination of both.

Other than poking someone in the chest, John has never touched anyone in anger. However, he definitely has a history of violent behavior. In his case, it's stage 1 violent behavior (regularly becoming argumentative and abusing others verbally) and possibly some stage 2 violent behavior (making verbal threats), but it's violent behavior nonetheless. John is a classic badgerer. He uses intimidation and verbal aggression to try to control others. As long as these tactics work, his violent behavior is unlikely to escalate to actual physical violence. The problem, however, comes when his badgering tactics *don't* work. And the more he uses such tactics, the sooner they will lose some (if not most) of their intended effect. John's colleagues may start to ignore his badgering. He may then raise its intensity level in an effort to maintain or regain control over them. Two things about this scenario are dangerous: (1) John is out of control, and (2) those who must bear the brunt of his violent badgering are likely at some point to lash back in self-defense.

Will John know that he's out of control? Probably not; that's the nature of the condition and of the defense mechanism of denial. Consider, though, that if he is unaware that he is out of control, he has no motivation to try to modulate his behavior and bring himself back under control. There are two common clues that a person is out of control and in denial about his or her inappropriate actions. (1) When reminded of or asked about a particular incident in which he or she really lost control and yelled at, threatened, or possibly even shoved another person, the out-of-control perpetrator reports no recollection of the event. (2) Almost immediately after badgering (and often humiliating) another person, the out-of-control perpetrator will interact with his or her victim as if nothing has happened—perhaps even making a joke or asking the person for a favor.

Besides denial, what else could be going on in the mind of the out-of-control badgerer? If the first clue is observed, the person has probably reacted so quickly and thoughtlessly in a badgering manner, and has come to consider this mode so normal, that he or she hardly even notices the behavior. If the second clue is observed, the person is so lacking in human empathy that it hasn't even occurred to him or her that the victim's feelings might have been hurt by the badgering (or worse—it does not occur to the perpetrator that the victim even has feelings; remember our discussion of dehumanization in chapter 2). *Narcissistic, arrogant,* and *antisocial* are all words that are used to describe such badgerers.

As for the victims of John's badgering, remember that one of the two situations in which people may become violent is when they are forced into a self-defense mode. John's colleagues aren't used to this kind of badgering behavior in the workplace. They're used to working out their disagreements and resolving their differences in a calmer, more professional way. At some point (if they haven't already), they may start taking John's attacks personally. And they may lash back in self-defense. They are as likely to be the instigator of physical violence in this situation as John is. And, of course, if one of his colleagues ever did hit John, he would no doubt see himself as the victim and put all the blame on the other person.

Again, looking at the total situation here, we'd have to say that there's currently a stage 1 threat of violence but that it could easily and quickly escalate to stage 2 or even stage 3.

Profile 5

The Employee with Severe Changes in Psychological Functioning

Betty is a 38-year-old cleaning lady at the community hospital. She lives at home with her elderly parents and apparently suffers from some mild mental or psychological disorder or disability, though no one she works with knows the exact details of her condition. Betty has never married and doesn't seem to have established any significant adult relationships. Her life revolves around her parents and the church they regularly attend. (Betty has sung in the church choir since she was seventeen.)

At the hospital where she works, Betty is considered a good worker although perhaps a bit "strange." Her supervisor says that she gets her work done and doesn't bother anyone. She works the evening shift, from 6:00 P.M. until 2:00 A.M. Taking the bus to work every day, she always arrives early, around 5:45. And at exactly 2:00, her father arrives by car to pick her up.

Although her co-workers don't know exactly what she suffers from, they do know not to upset her or demand too much from her. On one occasion, a co-worker was giving Betty some instructions, and Betty didn't seem to be paying attention. (She seemed, in fact, to be looking right through the person, as if she wasn't there.) When the co-worker attempted to get Betty's attention by saying, "Hello? Is anyone in there?" Betty responded by saying, "Don't make fun of me. I'll turn you into a turnip." On another occasion, Betty's supervisor found her sprawled across the desk in the office she was supposed to be cleaning, her ear pressed to the speakerphone on the desk. When the supervisor asked Betty what she was doing, Betty replied that she was listening to God. In fact, there were some intermittent words being broadcast over the hospital's paging system, the speaker for which was high up on the wall. When the supervisor tried to point to that speaker and explain what paging was, Betty became visibly upset. "You are a blasphemer, and you will burn in the eternal flames," she said. In addition to these two more prominent incidents, Betty regularly carries on conversations with imaginary persons. Her co-workers have learned to ignore her when she does so.

In recent weeks, Betty has become more and more irritable. She's constantly frowning and seems to be upset all the time. Also, for the first time in her nine years of working at the hospital, she has shown up late on several occasions. Moreover, her imaginary conversations are getting to be constant and never-ending. She can be heard blathering on continuously throughout her shift, and doesn't like to be interrupted for any reason. Occasionally she seems to be ranting in a somewhat threatening or violent way. One of her co-workers reported overhearing her saying something about offering a human sacrifice to God. Her supervisor has also been getting complaints from physicians who say their offices haven't been cleaned in days, that their wastebaskets are overflowing with paper. In all cases, the complaints were from persons whose offices Betty was supposed to have cleaned.

When Betty's supervisor confronted her about her failure to clean these offices, Betty's response was, "My pastor says my only responsibility is to have a clean soul." The supervisor tried to explain that the pastor was probably referring only to her spiritual responsibilities, but Betty just kept shaking her head and saying, "I don't think so." Eventually, the supervisor gave up trying to reason with Betty, and assigned another worker to check on her every hour to make sure she was getting her work done.

Betty is an employee with a mental or psychological disorder or disability. The exact diagnosis isn't important. What is important is that although her baseline functioning is adequate for her to do her job, that functioning has been noticeably slipping for the past several weeks. Her supervisor and co-workers have observed severe changes in Betty's psychological functioning. She hasn't acted out physically yet, and she hasn't made any overt threats either (the turnip comment was made several years ago, long before these recent changes). Still, it would be fair to say that she's exhibiting stage 1 violent behavior by her gross failure to comply with authority and social norms (showing up late for work, failing to clean the offices she's supposed to clean, and carrying on imaginary conversations constantly).

Persons who are mentally or psychologically challenged are not inherently violent. The danger, though, is that as their hold on reality diminishes, their potential for violent behavior increases. In addition, the potential for them to cause harm, whether to themselves or to others, through simple neglect also increases as they lose the ability to distinguish reality from fantasy. Assigning another worker to check up on Betty regularly is at best a temporary solution here. A better approach would be to call Betty's parents (with her permission, of course) to find out if anything in her home situation (or medical condition) has changed recently, and to inform them of her recent deterioration. Intervention on the part of her caretakers is more likely to lead to a permanent solution—which, in Betty's case, would be a return to her former level of timeliness, productivity, and general psychological functioning.

Profile 6

The Employee Demonstrating Decreased or Inconsistent Productivity

Jim is a 53-year-old computer programmer who has been working in his field for twenty-five years. At one time he was thought to be the best at what he does, but that was a long time ago. For the past few years his performance has been adequate but nothing stellar. (He attributes this decline to his age, and frequently jokes that he can't keep up with these young kids fresh out of college who like to stay up all night working.) Jim is married and has two children, both of whom are attending private colleges. It is well known around the office that his wife has had some serious (though unspecified) medical problems for the past year, and there have been rumors that Jim is facing financial difficulties, what with two kids in college, his wife no longer able to work, and medical bills mounting.

Although Jim's annual performance evaluations have been satisfactory, he often asks for more time or assistance from others to complete his assignments. Some of his colleagues have noticed that although he knows how to "look busy" when he's sitting at his computer, as often as not he might just be going over a personal to-do list or reviewing his personal finances on the company's spreadsheet program. Nevertheless, Jim is generally well liked around the office, so no one has spoken up about his difficulty concentrating on his work.

About three weeks ago, however, Jim's attentiveness to his work began to decline even further. He started showing up at work around 11:30 in the morning, and leaving around 2:30 or 3:00 in the afternoon. Moreover, it was hard to tell if he spent *any* time on work while he was there; he seemed to be making a lot of personal phone calls and working on his own personal projects on the computer. In the past Jim always had a reason for coming in late or leaving early, but lately he hasn't even bothered to try to explain his odd hours. He looks tired all the time, and when he leaves, he rushes off as if he's late for an urgent appointment. On a couple of occasions he's looked as if he was close to tears.

Jim's colleagues can check to see if he's read the e-mail messages they've sent him, and it sometimes takes him a week or more to look at a one-page memo. Meanwhile, his voice mailbox is full: No one can even leave him a message there. The only project he's currently working on has a deadline several months away; still, there's no evidence that he's making any progress on it at all. Occasionally, colleagues who are working on related projects will ask for his input on a particular question, and his response, if he makes one at all, will often be superficial if not outright wrong. In short, he doesn't seem to be properly tuned in to work.

Jim's productivity at work has declined precipitously. In and of itself, this fact is not necessarily indicative of violent potential. However, we would have to classify Jim's recent actions as stage 1 violence because of his failure to be at work during normal business hours and his gross negligence toward his work responsibilities (challenging authority). Moreover, his behavior of late could indicate several other problems or variables that *do* have a high correlation to further violence: depression, substance abuse, suicidal thoughts, and/or severe stress. Jim's supervisor needs to talk to him—about both his long-term slacking off and his recent total lack of productivity—to find out what the underlying problems or causes may be. Then these need to be addressed appropriately.

Profile 7
The Socially Isolated Employee Demonstrating Poor Peer Relationships

Andy is a 29-year-old repair technician working for the local power company. He dropped out of high school at the age of seventeen, just four months before his scheduled graduation. His explanation to his parents was, "They're all idiots at school, even the teachers. I'm only wasting time there." Sometime afterward, his parents learned that he had been a loner at school, that he had no real friends, and that most of his classmates considered him "weird."

Andy got his job with the power company shortly after dropping out of high school. He had an aptitude for technical knowledge and was good with his hands, so he quickly mastered his trade. When he was nineteen, he was considered for a promotion to supervisor. Had he gotten the promotion, he would have been the youngest supervisor in the company. But his managers backed away from the idea of promoting him when they learned that his co-workers dis-liked him strongly (several of them had stepped forward to say that they would quit before they would ever report to him).

Andy is unmarried and, as far as anyone knows, doesn't have any romantic or social life at all. He lives alone and never talks about any friends. He brings his lunch to work with him every day, and he always eats alone, in his pickup truck, regardless of the weather. He only speaks to his co-workers when it's absolutely necessary to do so; he never makes small talk or friendly conversation. Consequently, no one he works with knows much about him or particularly likes him. One thing they do know is that he subscribes to several sur-vivalist magazines; they've seen him reading them in his truck at lunchtime. Once, in fact, when Andy opened the door to his truck, one of his magazines slipped out and fell onto the street. A co-worker who was standing nearby bent down to pick it up, but before he had even touched it, Andy yanked the man's arm up and twisted it awkwardly behind his back. "You touch my stuff, and I'll break your arm," he said ominously. The man apologized and said he would never do it again. Andy let him go. The incident was never formally report-ed, so Andy was never disciplined for his actions.

During the twelve years that Andy has been working for this company, he has been transferred twenty-two times—mostly at his request, after his refusal to work with those he's been assigned to work with. Andy's inability to work with anyone puts his supervisors in a difficult position, since safety regulations require two technicians for most repair jobs. For the last six months Andy has been assigned to desk duty for the graveyard shift. He works from midnight to 8:00 A.M., taking calls from customers experiencing power outages during those hours. Surprisingly, until recently there have been no customer complaints about his performance. (There has also been a dramatic reduction in the number of complaints received during his shifts, and his managers don't know quite how to explain this.)

One recent morning, however, a supervisor received a call from a female customer who wanted to file a formal complaint against

Andy. About a year ago, Andy had been sent to her house to do some repairs. When the work was completed, Andy asked the woman if she wanted to attend some sort of local militia group meeting with him that weekend. The woman didn't feel particularly comfortable around Andy, and didn't like the idea of a militia group at all, so she politely declined. At first Andy just stood there staring at her. Then his work partner, who had been waiting for him outside, came back in to find out what was keeping him. The two repair technicians left, and the woman thought that that would be the end of it. But it wasn't. She received several calls and messages from Andy that week. He kept trying to get her to agree to go to the meeting with him, and she kept declining, politely. She was going to file a complaint at that time, she said, but when the day of the meeting passed, the calls from Andy stopped.

In the past few nights, however, they've started up again. Andy has been calling her late at night, between midnight and 1:00 A.M., or early in the morning, before 8:00. Using what she has described as a "really scary" tone, he's told her that they need to go to a minister right away and get married. "We're meant to be together," he keeps telling her. "You make good breeding stock, and God wants us to propagate the species."

Andy is a good example of an individual who exhibits more than one of the nine warning signs of potentially violent employees. He's definitely a loner, and his social isolation in and of itself poses a risk. He also has a history of a variety of violent behaviors, ranging from the ongoing sexual harassment that started a full year ago (stage 1) to the threats (stage 2) and assault (stage 3) on the co-worker who tried to pick up hismagazine for him. Moreover, he seems out of touch with reality given some of his comments to the female customer he's been harassing. This combination of a volatile history and delusional thinking is particularly dangerous. Andy's potential for violence is considerable; he should definitely be considered a stage 3 risk.

The key component of this profile is that Andy has been alienating everyone around him for years. The fact that he keeps to himself at work and doesn't talk much about his private life isn't the problem; nor is the fact that he reads survivalist magazines. The problem is that he has no friends whatsoever. So when he gets upset, frustrated, and angry—as we all inevitably do in our lives—to whom can he turn for support? Where can he vent his negative feelings? No one, and nowhere. Andy is a powder keg waiting to explode. And transferring him again isn't going to solve any problem; it's just going to shuffle it around a bit. Andy needs to be supervised much more closely, and he needs remedial training and/or discipline regarding his problematic relations with customers as well as co-workers.

Profile 8
The Employee Demonstrating Poor Personal Hygiene

Rita is a 32-year-old buyer for an upscale department store. Part of her job responsibility is to convince designers to allow her store exclusive rights to sell their clothing, and she has to be a good salesperson to do this. She's been with this store for three years, and everyone she works with likes and respects her. One of the things that always impresses people about Rita is her professional appearance. Her hair is always styled, her makeup perfect, and her nails freshly manicured. She wears all the latest fashions, and is cordial and professional with everyone she deals with. She is in many ways a walking advertisement for the store, and her superiors have called her a rising star within her department.

Fridays are a casual-dress day in Rita's department, though even her "casual" outfits are neater and more professional than most people's regular attire. For the past two weeks, though, Rita has been wearing dirty, old jeans and several layers of wrinkled cotton shirts to work. She's worn no makeup, and looks like she hasn't been sleeping well, with dark circles under her eyes. Her hair doesn't even seem to be brushed much less styled; she just ties it up into a sloppy pony-tail, as if it's a weekend morning and she's at home cleaning the house or yard. One day a friend at work asked her if she was sick or some-thing, and Rita's reply was, "Not that I know of." "What's with the bad hair day then?" the woman asked. Rita shrugged. "I'm tired of spend-ing so much time taking care of my hair. I guess I just didn't feel like it today."

On Monday, Rita and her immediate supervisor had an impor-tant appointment with a designer they were trying to sign to an exclusive contract. But when the supervisor stopped by Rita's office to check on some details of their presentation, she found Rita staring out the window as if she were on drugs or something. Moreover, she was appalled at Rita's sloppy appearance: She looked as if she'd just rolled out of bed and was wearing what she'd slept in. Not only that, but she had noticeably bad breath. When the supervisor asked Rita if she'd forgotten about the meeting, Rita said, "No, I'm all set for it." Her usual warmth and enthusiasm were completely gone. The super-visor decided that Rita must be having some personal troubles and decided to give her a break about it. She did, however, reschedule the meeting with the designer to avoid making a poor presentation.

Rita's personal hygiene and grooming continued to deteriorate. Some of her colleagues began making jokes about how bad she smelled, and saying things like "look what the cat dragged in today." And several of the designers that Rita worked with had commented to her managers about her as well, wondering if everything was okay with her.

The key component to notice here is not that Rita was wear-ing jeans instead of designer fashions, or that she wasn't wear-ing makeup, or that her hair was in a ponytail instead of some other style. There's a wide range of clothing and personal grooming styles that are acceptable in the workplace. However, there are certain *minimal* standards of personal hygiene that we all must adhere to in different areas of our lives. Showing up for a job in which she represents the image of the store she works for, dressed as if she's just been raking leaves on a rainy Saturday, is inappropriate. Wearing dirty clothes and failing to bathe and brush her teeth regularly, so that her body odor and bad breath are noticeable to others, is offensive.

As much as anything else, Rita's poor personal hygiene is cause for concern because it represents such a drastic change from her normal pattern of behavior. The Rita everyone knew and liked obviously cared a lot what people thought of her, because she spent a lot of time grooming and dressing herself to appear attractive and professional to others. What has happened to change that? Does Rita no longer care what others think of her? Does she no longer care about herself? Is she ill? Does she have a drug problem? Is she undergoing severe stress for reasons unknown to her co-workers? Could she possibly be depressed or maybe even suicidal? Any one or more of these explanations could apply.

Rita hasn't acted out yet, either physically or verbally. But her failure to conform to minimal standards of personal hygiene could be considered challenging authority, and she's beginning to alienate co-workers, customers, and clients. We'd have to say that she's exhibiting stage 1 violent behavior. And depending on what the underlying problem(s) may be, her potential for further violence could be even greater.

Profile 9
The Employee Demonstrating Drastic Changes in Personality

Jim, the 53-year-old computer programmer whose productivity declined sharply, and Rita, the 32-year-old department store buyer who suddenly started demonstrating poor personal hygiene, are both good examples of employees demonstrating drastic changes in personality. *Personality,* in this context, refers to the totality of a person's behavioral and emotional characteristics. Again, the thing to remember is that most of us tend to be fairly consistent in our behaviors, both in different places and at different times. Most of us, in fact, really are creatures of habit: We tend to do the same things, day after day, week after week, and we tend to interact with people in similar ways from one day or week to the next. So when Jim starts showing up to work at 11:30 and leaving at 2:30, or when Rita starts showing up wearing dirty, inappropriate attire and no makeup, with her hair unwashed and her teeth unbrushed, something's amiss.

Furthermore, notice in both these profiles that it wasn't just the productivity or personal grooming that declined; their emotional state and their interactions with others deteriorated as well. They both looked tired and despondent, as if they hadn't slept well lately and were having difficulty dealing with some serious personal problems. Jim was slow to read his mail, offered no excuse for his absences, and sometimes seemed on the verge of tears. Rita stared out her office window as if she were on drugs, and whereas previously she had been friendly and enthusiastic in her dealings with others, now she was nonplussed and flat in her affect.

The things people say often provide clues to their emotional and psychological state. Rita's response about why her hair was so slovenly ("I guess I just didn't feel like [taking care of] it today") could be indicative of a passing mood or of a deep underlying problem. And if Jim started swearing around the office regularly, for the first time that anyone could remember, this would probably suggest (or confirm) that he's in considerable distress.

The employee demonstrating drastic changes in personality would probably be classified as exhibiting stage 1 violent behavior (as both Jim and Rita were), though this would depend on the particulars of what they said and did. Recall our earlier example of an employee demonstrating drastic changes in personality, which we provided in chapter 3—Rob, the manager who suddenly began sexually harassing his assistant, Leslie (stage 1), conveying unwanted sexual attention in written format (stage 2), and ultimately assaulted her sexually (stage 3). Perhaps he had a drug problem that no one knew about, or was losing his hold on reality. Whatever the cause, you can see how drastic changes in personality can quickly lead to an escalation of violent behaviors.

Prevention
and
Intervention

In this section we will outline the steps companies must take in order to reduce the number and severity of violent incidents. We will discuss policies and procedures as well as tools to use to keep the workplace safe. We will also focus on preventing major acts of violence by intervening early with an emphasis on understanding situations that could easily result in injury. Finally, we will describe the specific characteristics of people who present a higher risk of violence, along with some general principles for intervention, since recognition of potentially violent employees is the key to prevention.

chapter 5

Prevention Policies and Procedures

Over and over again we hear about companies increasing security or calling for emergency board meetings *after* a violent incident has occurred. While these actions are certainly understandable, and preferable to doing nothing at all, they place the organization in a perpetual reactive mode. Very often, however, the morale of the employees and their ability to be productive without concern for their safety has been permanently damaged by the incident.

We have known for quite some time that preparation reduces anxiety. Recall when you were in school and there was a major exam. How did you feel walking into the classroom when you were *not* prepared, when you had *not* read the material to be covered on the test? If you were like most students, you had that sinking feeling in your stomach, perhaps you were short of breath,

---

Six Components for an Effective Prevention Plan

1. A workplace violence policy

2. An emergency response plan

3. A crisis management team

4. Training for first-level supervisors/managers

5. Vendor compliance

6. Customer compliance

---

and maybe you even fantasized about the instructor falling ill and being unable to come to class. Compare those feelings to the feelings you experienced when you *had* read all the material and felt confident that you were well prepared for the exam.

So it is in dealing with difficult situations and people at work. When you feel confident that your company is prepared to deal appropriately with whatever violent behavior may arise—even (and perhaps especially) if it's only stage 1 violent behavior—then you don't have to be anxious about the possibility of more extreme incidents of violence. That's why it's crucial that every organization develop the necessary policies and procedures, both for preventing workplace violence and for intervening should an incident occur.

In this chapter we will outline those policies and procedures that are oriented toward *preventing* workplace violence. There are six components of an effective workplace violence prevention plan. These six components are listed in the accompanying box above; they also provide the organizing framework for this chapter.

A Workplace Violence Policy

Before you think, "Oh, no, not another policy," consider the following: Most people will follow the instructions and expectations of others when those instructions and expectations are made clear. Without an official, written workplace violence *policy,* an employee behaving in an unacceptable manner (for example, swearing at others) is not technically breaking any rule. Furthermore, in the event of an incident in which someone gets hurt, expect that there will be a lawsuit. In defending this lawsuit, you or your company will be asked, "Were you aware that the latest thinking suggests that *all* companies need a policy forbidding certain behaviors? Can you produce for us a copy of your workplace violence policy?"

To be effective, a workplace violence policy must state clearly that the company is taking a proactive approach to violence, and that it will tolerate neither violent behavior nor any behavior that is known to have a high correlation to violence. The policy must clearly state what the consequences are for breaching its rules. It must also give examples of what is to be considered violence. Figure 1 provides a brief but good example of an effective workplace violence policy.

Information Campaign

When administrators painstakingly develop a violence prevention policy and simply bury it in a manual on a shelf, it serves little purpose to the organization and its employees. Once a policy is developed, the company must embark on a campaign to ensure that everyone in the organization becomes aware of it and clearly understands it. Some of the methods that have been effective in announcing the policy to current employees include the following:

- Companywide e-mail memos announcing the new policy
- Bulletin board notices
- Flyers inside of pay envelopes
- Abbreviated messages on pay stubs referring employees to the policy
- Department- and companywide voice mail messages

Making prospective employees or new hires aware of the policy is also important. Some organizations have accomplished this by doing the following:

- Including the policy statement as part of the employment application
- Requiring new hires to read and sign the policy before the organization tenders a job offer
- Teaching violence awareness as part of new employee orientation

In addition to these methods, it is important to make sure that no one in the organization becomes complacent. Including awareness of violence policies and procedures on any examinations for promotion is one way to accomplish this. Also, periodic (even quarterly) reminders are a great way to demonstrate to all in the company that the administration takes the risks of violence very seriously. Do not allow violence awareness to simply be a "flavor of the month."

An Emergency Response Plan

When a crisis occurs, lives can be saved if there is an action plan in place. The worst time to try to figure out what to do is when you are faced with a potentially deadly situation. Your emergency response plan will guide the behavior of your employees during an emergency situation. Make sure that your plan includes information on alternate exits in your building and a

To: All Employees

From: Human Resources

Re: Workplace Violence Policy

It is the purpose of this policy to communicate to all employees that this organization will take a proactive stance to ensure a safe working environment for all employees. It is every employee's responsibility to assist in establishing and maintaining a violence-free work environment. Therefore, each employee is expected to report those incidents that constitute violence.

This organization will have zero tolerance for acts of violence and threats of violence. Without exception, acts and threats of violence are not permitted. All such acts and threats, even those made in apparent jest, will be taken seriously, and will lead to discipline up to and including termination. Possession of non-work-related weapons on company premises and at company-sponsored events shall constitute a threat of violence. A threat shall also include, but not be limited to, any indication of intent to harm a person or damage company property. Threats may be direct or indirect, and they may be communicated verbally or nonverbally. The following are examples of threats and acts that shall be considered violent:

- Saying, "Do you want to see your next birthday?" (an indirect threat)
- Writing, "Employees who kill their supervisors have the right idea" (an indirect threat)
- Saying, "I'm going to punch your lights out" (a direct threat)
- Making a hitting motion or obscene gesture (a nonverbal threat)
- Displaying weapons (an extreme threat)
- Stalking or otherwise forcing undue attention on someone, whether romantic or hostile (an extreme threat)
- Taking actions likely to cause bodily harm or property damage (acts of violence)

Figure 1
Example of a Workplace Violence Policy

mechanism for determining how many of your employees were actually in the building. Also, make sure that your employees know that once they are safely out of harm's way, they need to notify administrators of that fact. These two steps can be helpful to police in determining how many people remain in the building during a crisis.

Do you know what you would do if you heard that a person wielding a gun was in your building? Would you head for an exit? Would you hide under your desk? If you are responsible for others in your organization, how would you know if they all exited the building safely? Would you be able to give the police an exact count of which workers were in today and who was out on leave? If you have not thought through these questions, your emergency response plan needs work. All organizations need to have an emergency response plan, and all employees need to be aware of it. And if your company is one of the many companies that has *not* put the time into developing an emergency response plan, you need a personal plan for yourself.

A Crisis Management Team

The crisis management team is responsible for oversight of the company's violence prevention program. The team should consist of six to eight individuals. Their specific disciplines can vary; however, some of the suggested departmental representatives include personnel from security, human resources, legal, and labor relations.

In addition to administering the violence prevention program, the crisis management team has three other primary responsibilities:

1. Coaching supervisors/managers

2. Tracking violent incidents

3. Serving as a liaison to relevant external organizations

Coaching Supervisors/Managers

Members of the crisis management team must become the organization's in-house experts on issues pertaining to violence. In this capacity, the crisis management team provides support to first-level supervisors and managers responsible for those individuals causing the most concern. These supervisors and managers will consult with the crisis management team members, and together they will make a determination regarding the threat level and course of action required to deal with the individuals in question. Each member of the crisis management team must therefore be well versed in company policies (regarding termination, leaves of absence, suspensions, etc.) as well as knowledgeable about available resources (such as health insurance, the company's employee assistance program, fitness for duty evaluations, etc.) for dealing with potentially violent employees.

Tracking Violent Incidents

One of the most problematic realities in most companies is the lack of documentation of incidents of violent behavior. Consider the following scenario:

> Ben, who works under the supervision of Mary, has exhibited several stage 1 outbursts. But Mary is a competent supervisor and manages to defuse each of Ben's outbursts. She decides that no further action is necessary. After six months, however, Mary is promoted. Ben now reports to Sam. Under Sam's supervision, Ben exhibits several more stage 1 outbursts and one stage 2 outburst. Because Sam is also a very keen supervisor, he too is able to calm Ben down and defuse the situations. Again, no further action is taken. After a year, Sam is promoted and Ben now reports to Sally. On Sally's first day in the office, she says something to Ben that he takes as criticism. He blows up and pushes Sally; she falls and injures her wrist. When Sally gives her statement to the police, she comments that Ben's behavior came "out of the blue."

Such a scenario is played out in the workplace on a daily basis. Is there any liability for the company in this scenario? What could have prevented Sally's injury? Who, besides Ben, shared in the responsibility for it? Both Mary and Sam had known of Ben's violent history, and each had a responsibility to warn others. As first-level supervisors, and thus the eyes and ears of the company, Mary and Sam had a responsibility to inform *their* supervisors of Ben's inappropriate behavior. And the unfortunate legal reality is that company administrators, whether or not they knew directly of Ben's behavior, also share in the responsibility for Sally's injury.

Much of the "dropping of the ball" that occurred in this scenario can be reduced when the organization implements a mechanism for tracking violent incidents. Simply put, this mechanism requires supervisors/managers to document any and all incidents of violence, even those that are successfully resolved. This documentation is passed on to the crisis management team, whose members then review the incident and the actions taken by the supervisor to determine if the actions taken were appropriate. The crisis management team then maintains records of all such incidents. With these records, the crisis management team can easily spot an individual whose violent behavior is escalating, and intervene appropriately *before* things get out of hand.

Serving as a Liaison to Relevant External Organizations

Another responsibility of the crisis management team is to interact with experts and resources outside of the organization. The requirement here is to develop and maintain relationships with contact individuals who may provide assistance in times of crisis. Some of those contacts will include law enforcement agents, mental health care professionals, and local media. It is often most efficient to designate one member of the crisis management team to serve as external liaison for the company.

The external liaison is responsible for making certain that all required resources are available to the company and its employees. The external liaison is also required to control the information flow to and from the organization. For example, if an individual who has been harassing members of your company is arrested, the external liaison would be responsible for reporting to the administration on how the case is proceeding in the courts. Additionally, when there is a major incident that prompts media attention, the liaison would be the media spokesperson.

Training for First-Level Supervisors/Managers

As we have stated above, first-level supervisors and managers serve as the eyes and ears of the organization. More than mid- and upper-level managers, first-level supervisors and managers are the ones interacting with employees, customers, and clients on a regular (often daily) basis. Therefore they are the ones more likely to notice potential threats of violence before the behavior escalates to dangerous levels. In order to help prevent workplace violence, first-level supervisors and managers need to receive training in the following four areas:

1. Early threat recognition
2. Intervention techniques for stage 1 and stage 2 violence
3. Emergency response procedures for stage 3 violence
4. Reporting and documenting violent incidents

Early Threat Recognition

All first-level supervisors and managers must be able to identify those individuals and behaviors that have been shown to have a high correlation to violent behavior. Additionally, all first-level supervisors and managers must be able to correctly identify the stage of violent behavior they have witnessed (or that was reported to them) and the corresponding warning signs. The key here is that the supervisor must be aware of when the individual is a potential versus an active threat.

The ability to identify those individuals and circumstances that have a high correlation to violence comes only through training. Early threat recognition training must include commonly seen scenarios and detailed descriptions of behavioral cues to be on the lookout for. When first-level supervisors and managers are trained to identify these behaviors, then and only then can they act effectively as the eyes and ears of the organization in preventing workplace violence.

Intervention Techniques for Stage 1 and Stage 2 Violence

All first-level supervisors and managers should be trained in early intervention techniques. While first-level supervisors and managers are not expected to handle these situations without support from the crisis management team, they should be able to defuse active incidents until further assistance can be summoned. This training should consist of both verbal and nonverbal techniques for defusing violent behavior.

There have been many incidents in which an improperly trained individual attempted to intervene and actually made the situation worse (for example, the violent behavior escalated). First-level supervisors and managers must understand the nature of a "win-win" resolution and be able to implement one. Very often, supervisors are accustomed to having people follow their instructions simply by virtue of their being "in charge." In a potentially violent scenario, however, a manager with an "in-charge" attitude could very well be the excuse the perpetrator seeks to rationalize a violent behavior. Also, it is important that each manager understand that defusing a violent situation is separate and distinct from disciplining the violent employee. In other words, although the aggressor may deserve discipline, the most important concern while he or she is acting out is that the situation be resolved without any injury or loss of life.

Emergency Response Procedures for Stage 3 Violence

As we have described, stage 3 violent behavior is actual physical violence. The supervisor/manager must be able to identify this behavior, and must immediately implement the emergency response plan. Attempting to defuse stage 3 violent behavior is ill-advised, for the person you're dealing with is not likely to respond to reason. First-level supervisors and managers (and, indeed, all responsible persons) have three responsibilities when they encounter stage 3 violent behavior.

1. *Get out of harm's way.* This may involve leaving the building or even hiding under a desk. Only you can decide what's safest under the circumstances.

2. *Warn others.* We have a moral obligation to warn other potential victims of the danger at hand. However, this obligation does not require you to put your own safety at risk. What it *does* require is that as you yourself are getting out of harm's way, you alert others whom you encounter to do the same.

3. *Contact the authorities.* Once you've gotten yourself out of harm's way and warned others of the danger at hand, you must contact the appropriate authorities so that they can intervene. The appropriate authorities may be in-house security or local law enforcement agencies. *Do not attempt to intervene on your own with an individual exhibiting stage 3 violent behavior.*

Reporting and Documenting Violent Incidents

Each company should develop and distribute an incident report form; and first-level supervisors and managers should be trained regarding its use. The form should be relatively short, to help encourage people to use it. It should include spaces for reporting the following information, as relevant:

- Who: the victim(s) as well as the perpetrator
- What: the specific violent behaviors observed or reported, and what intervention (if any) took place
- When: date and time
- Where: in a particular office or common area of the building, on the grounds, or away from company property (but while working)
- Why: historical problems, personal differences, and/or any explanations offered

An incident report form should be completed by the first-level supervisor or manager directly responsible for the perpetrator, and then forwarded to the crisis management team. This mechanism allows the crisis management team to track incidents and individuals of particular concern. Furthermore, it is important that these forms be completed even if the violent or potentially violent situation or behavior was successfully resolved, so that the crisis management team can follow up with the problem individual, and so that the company has a written record should that person ever act out again.

Vendor Compliance

There is a tendency to assume that all workplace violence originates with employees. However, this is not true. A significant percentage of violence occurring in the workplace takes place at the hands of individuals who are not employees of the organization. Therefore, it is essential that organizations require their vendors to follow the same policy as their employees. This is simple enough to implement once the organization has adopted a workplace violence policy. See the statement below:

> [Company Name] is committed to establishing and maintaining a violence-free work environment. In keeping with this objective, we are requiring that all vendors and contractors and their employees observe and adhere to our workplace violence policy.

When entering into any agreement with a contractor or vendor, simply include a statement such as this one along with your company's workplace violence policy.

Customer Compliance

With employees and vendors, you have some leverage to get them to observe and adhere to your policy on workplace violence: If they don't commit to doing so, you won't offer them jobs or give them work. With customers, you don't have quite the same leverage. However, there are concrete steps you can take to *encourage* customers to behave appropriately—and to *discourage* them (especially irate customers) from acting inappropriately. Three such steps are described below:

1. *Post signs.* Posted signs are effective in communicating to your customers how you expect them to conduct themselves. For example, "At [Company Name], your safety and ours is our most important concern. Therefore, we respectfully request that you refrain from using aggressive language and behavior." People are used to seeing signs and following the instructions on them. Additionally, signs offer a distraction when customers are waiting in a long line.

2. *Install mirrors.* It may seem strange, but mirrors do have the effect of helping us keep our behavior in check. Most

people don't see themselves as they are acting out—and are usually embarrassed when they do. Mirrors call attention to oneself and how one's behavior appears to others.

3. *Hire security guards.* Security guards are often overlooked in discussions on customer violence. However, they do help to deter inappropriate behavior.

chapter 6

Prevention Tools

A potential problem area for most companies is negligent hiring, such as when an individual with a history of violent behavior is hired anyway. Negligent hiring is often a result of cursory screening of applicants. One of the most effective methods of detecting troubled individuals is to check the backgrounds of all applicants. As we have discussed, problem individuals tend to take/make trouble wherever they go. It is important, therefore, to get as thorough an understanding as possible of who a person is *before* hiring him or her. There are a number of preemployment tools you can use to screen applicants; there are also a number of *post*employment tools you can use to deal with problem employees who have slipped through the screening process (or who were hired before the preemployment tools were used effectively). These various tools are listed in the

---

Prevention Tools

Preemployment Tools—for Screening Applicants
- Résumés
- References
- Work history
- Psychological testing
- Interviews

Postemployment Tools—for Dealing with Problem Employees
- Termination
- Restraining orders
- Surveillance

---

accompanying box above. In this chapter we will describe each of them in turn.

Résumés

It is fairly well accepted that much of what is written in résumés is designed to make one's experiences appear more significant and varied than they actually are. An unpublished exit poll from a 1995 job fair found that up to 85 percent of prospective employees exaggerated on their résumés. However, a distinction must be made between exaggerating and outright lying. Consider the following example:

> Mary attended a prestigious private women's university in the Northeast. She received her B.A. degree in business with a specialization in marketing. For eight months during her senior year, she interned in the marketing division of a well-known Fortune 100 company. Her intern sponsor was a mid-level manager in that division.

Mary attended marketing meetings, mostly to take notes for her sponsor, and on occasion was allowed to participate in the discus-. sion. During her internship, the organization landed a major contract with an international corporation. This contract was record-setting in its breadth and cost, and made international headlines. Mary's sponsor was the main catalyst for the signing of this contract, and Mary gained valuable insight in witnessing the evolution of the deal. Upon graduation, Mary applied for a job at another Fortune 100 company and described her "internship" (though she didn't call it that) in the following way: "As a marketing assistant, I participated in the procurement of the largest contract in the company's history, and contributed to the development of marketing strategy."

Because Mary has failed to mention that she was an intern, and that she mostly only took notes, she has exaggerated her experiences. However, it is well known that students use their internships partly to build their résumés, and technically she did participate on the marketing team. So she hasn't really lied. Now compare the above to the following example:

Fred attended a small, unaccredited community college. While he was a student there, he was allowed to audit several courses at the more prestigious neighboring university. However, he did not receive grades for these audited courses, and he was not considered a matriculated student. Upon graduation from the community college, Fred listed on his résumé that his B.A. was from the prestigious university where all he had done was audit a few courses.

Fred has lied—there's no doubt about it. He hasn't just padded his résumé by putting an exaggerated spin on his experiences; he has claimed to have earned a degree from a prestigious university where he was never even a matriculated student. This is unacceptable. The danger to the prospective employer is that if Fred has lied to them already, what will he do a month, six months, or a year from now? He can't be trusted. And the only way the company would be able to find this out ahead of time (and thereby avoid making a bad hire), would be by questioning the validity of the résumés of all their applicants.

The company could call the registrar of the university to confirm that the applicant was actually a student there and actually graduated. In our examples, Mary would pass this test or checkpoint, but Fred would not. The company could also attempt to determine during the interview process just how much the applicant might have exaggerated his or her experience. Again, Mary would probably pass this checkpoint (yes, she exaggerated a little, but not to an unacceptable degree), whereas Fred—unless he was a particularly skillful and creative liar—would probably fail it. (The problem with lies is that they engender further lies, and the liar soon gets caught in his or her own web of prevarication.)

As soon as the company determines that an applicant has lied on his or her résumé or employment application, the company should reject that applicant—or terminate the employee if he or she has already been hired.

References

Prospective employees should be able to provide personal and professional references when requested—either names and phone numbers of persons the company can call, or written letters of recommendation. These references should then be able to speak about the individual's character, personality, and morality. When the F.B.I. and other security-conscious organizations investigate prospective employees, they routinely request personal references. Often, they will even talk to neighbors to get a feel for the habits and tendencies of a prospective employee. Obviously, most employers will not and cannot go to these same lengths; however, even written references can give insight into the individual's ability to get along with others.

Imagine someone who's capable of stage 3 violent behavior. This person would probably have some difficulty getting anyone other than a family member to attest to his or her ability to get along with others and suitability for the job in question. If you ask for a reference or written letter of recommendation, you might screen out such a potential bad hire just by asking for something that the person is unable to provide. And if you follow up by calling the references or carefully reading the letters of recommendation, you're likely to find evidence of the person's violent history or potential. There's no guarantee that you'll screen out every potentially violent employee this way, but you will be able to screen out many of them.

Work History

Very often former employers, feeling the threat of lawsuits hanging over their heads, fail to specify why an individual is no longer employed with the company. For years the conventional legal advice has been that former employers should limit the information they release to bare-bones facts: job title, function, dates of employment, and wage or salary paid. More recently, companies find themselves facing another potential lawsuit: that of failure to warn. Increasingly, individuals as well as organizations are asking the courts to force former employers to share in the responsibility when a former employee becomes violent after having been given a good or neutral recommendation despite a history of violent behavior. Consider the following example:

> Tom, who works at company A, has been behaving in a threatening manner. On one occasion he actually tells his supervisor that he has a gun and threatens to use it. After this incident, Tom is fired because

his behavior was a violation of company policy. Tom then seeks employment at company B. When asked why he left his last employer, he says it was because there was no possibility of promotion there. When company B calls company A to ask about Tom's work history, company A confirms the facts of Tom's employment there but makes no mention of his violent history. Company B hires Tom. Six months down the road, Tom shoots a co-worker at his new job.

Was there a duty to warn? Is company A legally liable in some way for Tom's violent action? There has been much debate among human resource professionals about this. However, many organizations have decided that releasing *accurate* negative information about former employees is preferable to playing dumb and being sued later. (One possible solution to the dilemma regarding whether or not to release negative information about a former employee: Company A could inform Tom at the time of his termination that if a future prospective employer calls to ask about his work history, they *will* provide information about his violent behavior. This warning may keep Tom from listing company A as a reference or even as a former employer. Consult with your corporate counsel regarding the best strategy for your company to follow.)

In addition to past episodes of violence, there are other red flags in the area of work history. Recruiters have known for years that individuals who move from one employer to the next in quick succession can be major risks. The theory has been that time and money put into training this individual will *not* be returned in productivity. Now it is also clear that these individuals often have a difficult time establishing themselves on the job. They frequently have difficulty relating to others (a warning sign) and sometimes challenge authority (stage 1 violent behavior). Therefore, be sure to thoroughly explore and investigate the work history of each new applicant. When you detect a pattern of rapidly moving from one job to the next, ask the applicant to explain this pattern—and be sure to ask the applicant's former employers about his or her reason(s) for leaving those jobs.

Psychological Testing

Psychological testing can provide an accurate determination of an individual's stability and functioning level. This type of testing can often detect problems dealing with authority, difficulty following rules, poor interpersonal skills, aggressive tendencies, and other traits that might be inappropriate in the workplace. In addition, psychological testing very often yields information about how well or how poorly an individual adapts to stressors such as change, and how flexible or rigid an individual is. This information can then be used to project expected performance in your environment. For example, a rigid and inflexible individual would probably have problems in an unstructured environment where things are constantly in flux. It is important to remember that psychological testing is best used to screen *out* undesirable employees, as opposed to screening *in* good workers. There are other, more appropriate methods for evaluating a person's potential productivity.

There are certain industries and professions that routinely use psychological testing to screen applicants. There are also some states that widely regulate the use of psychological testing. Your human resources or personnel department should be able to clarify your state's laws on the use of such testing. If it is legal to utilize these methods, it is highly recommended that your organization do so. They are effective screening tools.

Interviews

Once a prospective employee passes all of the pencil-and-paper screening methods, the final screening step should be a face-to-face meeting. Moreover, this interview should *not* be a mere formality or "rubber-stamp" step in the hiring process. Instead, the focus should be on comparing the information the applicant gave on paper to what he or she presents orally in the meeting. Be on the lookout for the following negative and positive clues:

- Inconsistencies in information provided
- Attention to social norms (attire, eye contact, handshakes, etc.)
- Timeliness to the interview
- A reluctance to discuss work history
- An unwillingness to acknowledge weaknesses or past mistakes

Paying attention to the above factors will help you to assess the applicant's professionalism and sense of responsibility. The discussion of the applicant's weaknesses is particularly telling. No one is good at everything. The applicant's willingness or unwillingness to acknowledge that there are areas in which he or she needs to improve (and/or has made mistakes in the past) indicates a tendency (or lack thereof) to blame others for his or her own shortcomings. It also says something about the person's insight into him- or herself. Imagine asking an applicant the following: "Mr. Smith, you appear on paper to be the perfect candidate for the job. What would you say is the one area in which you most need to improve?" The well-adjusted person would *not* go into a ten-minute self-deprecating speech. However, the well-adjusted person *would* describe for you an area in which he or she has yet to acquire or develop some particular knowledge, experience, or skill that would be useful in his or her chosen profession. "Well, I would like to be able to say that I'm a computer whiz. But the fact is that I am barely computer-literate. I do, however, hope to really improve in that area." This answer shows a healthy insight into oneself as well as a desire to grow. Contrast that response with this one: "Well, to tell you the truth, I can't think of an area that I'm not good in." This answer indicates a lack of insight into oneself and potentially suggests an attitude of, "It must be someone else who's at fault, because I don't make mistakes." Which is a dangerous attitude indeed.

Termination

Sometimes even with the appropriate preemployment screening mechanisms in place, problem situations evolve that an organization cannot allow to continue. In many of these situations, terminating the employee to remove the violent threat is the most sensible alternative. The assumption here is that the company has in place the necessary policies to support the termination. Once again, the company's workplace violence policy must clearly prohibit violent behavior and give examples of which behaviors will be deemed violent. Furthermore, a termination must always be handled with respect toward the employee, in a manner that preserves the dignity of all persons involved.

When to Terminate

Termination as a result of violent behavior should occur as soon after the violent incident as possible. This recommendation comes from theories on discipline which suggest that discipline must be certain, severe, and swift. The *certainty* of the discipline serves as a deterrent to others. It makes it clear that inappropriate behavior will not be tolerated or overlooked. The *severity* of the discipline helps to make others weigh the cost of their acts. And finally, in the case of violent behavior, the *swiftness* of the discipline serves to protect those who remain in the workplace. At the same time, however, the above considerations need to be tempered with the need for adequate time for planning. That is to say, a termination proceeding should *not* be initiated until there is a plan in place that allows for the safe resolution of the problem. It is better to delay slightly in order to develop such a plan than to move forward unprepared.

How to Terminate

There is a tendency to fire problem employees at the end of the workday on Friday, to avoid giving them any opportunity to sabotage the company. Company administrators routinely wait until Friday at 5:00 P.M. so that the fired employee doesn't have any time to steal company property, sabotage equipment, or negatively influence other personnel. While this concern for company security is admirable, it is misplaced.

When a person is fired at 5:00 P.M. on Friday, he or she then has all weekend to stew over the perceived unfairness and mistreatment. "I can't believe they did this to me. After all my years of service, I deserve better than this." These are common thoughts. Sometimes as the weekend goes on, worries and anxieties arise and multiply. "What will happen to the money I have paid into the retirement fund? Are my health insurance benefits canceled already? What will my boss say when someone calls to check on my employment history? Will I ever be able to get another job?" These are the kinds of questions a recently fired person will ask of him- or herself. Where does he or she get the answers to these questions at 5:00 P.M. on a Friday? Usually there are no answers at that time; there's no one to even listen to the questions. This helps explain how panic can set in over the weekend. This is not to say that terminating an employee on Friday at 5:00 P.M. *causes* that individual to act out violently on Monday. Remember, this is a person who was fired *because of* his or her preexisting potential for violence. However, depending on how it's handled, the termination can act as a triggering event. Along with the panic the person may experience, the circumstances (or the mere fact) of the termination can be the rationalization used to justify subsequent violent behavior.

A preferable procedure would involve terminating the employee as early in the week as possible and as early in the day as possible. This gives the terminated employee an opportunity to get answers to at least some of the inevitable questions, and may allow him or her to deal with the termination and move on much more quickly. Our guidelines for termination include the following specific steps:

1. Document the inappropriate behavior.

2. Confer with representatives from human resources, personnel, the crisis management team, and in-house security.

3. Develop a plan for informing the employee of the termination. This plan should include details concerning who will attend the meeting, who will conduct the meeting, where the meeting will take place, and who will be standing by in case the problem employee begins to act out.

4. Gather all information regarding wages, health insurance, retirement monies, unused leave, and any other financial matters about which the employee may have questions, *before* the meeting. Be prepared to answer these questions. If at all possible, have the employee's final paycheck ready, and give it to him or her at the meeting.

5. Schedule the meeting with the employee (again, preferably early in the week, early in the day).

6. Explain to the employee what company resources (if any) will remain available to him or her.

7. Explain how the company will handle reference checks from prospective subsequent employers.

8. Allow the employee to vent his or her feelings within reason (if the employee becomes abusive, however, terminate the meeting at once).

9. Explain to the employee that his or her personal belongings will be packed up and mailed or delivered to him or her within one day (or two at the most).

10. Obtain all pass cards, company I.D., badges, and keys from the employee.

11. Designate one person as the contact person should the employee have any further questions. It is preferable that this contact person be in security or perhaps human resources or personnel. Give the person's name and work number to the employee, and explain that this individual is the only appropriate contact person from now on. If the question involves another department, explain that the contact person will relay any questions and responses.

12. Explain to the employee that because of safety concerns, he or she is not to attempt to gain entry or access to any company property.

When the Employee Is Off-Site

Often, an employee that the company needs to terminate is already off-site for one reason or another. The employee may have been placed on leave following an inappropriate act, or may have stormed out of the building after an altercation. In any event, the organization must use this time to develop a termination strategy. A common mistake is to bring the violent individual back into the work environment to terminate him or her. However, this violates security considerations. Remember, this employee is being terminated because of the safety risk posed to others. Do *not* bring him or her back into the workplace.

We offer the following guidelines for terminating an employee who is already off-site:

1. Contact representatives from the crisis management team and/or human resources, personnel, and security. Discuss and document the offending behaviors.

2. Pack up the employee's personal belongings.

3. Draft a letter to the employee. Include in this letter all the information you would have communicated in a face-to-face meeting: the inappropriate behaviors that led to termination, the effective date of the termination, information about all financial matters and health insurance, how references will be handled, and instructions on whom to contact for additional information or questions.

4. Be sure to have others read the letter before it goes out to ensure that it is complete and appropriately worded. Try to make sure that the letter conveys compassion and concern for the employee and not just cold, hard facts about the termination.

5. Send the letter along with the employee's final paycheck via certified mail.

6. On the day that the letter is scheduled to arrive, follow up with a phone call to the terminated employee. This is important because the person will want to vent his or her feelings and should be given an opportunity to do so. However, make sure that the individual who makes the phone call knows exactly what is in the letter so that the information conveyed is consistent.

7. Mail the employee's personal belongings to his or her residence.

Restraining Orders

Temporary restraining orders are legally supported requirements that an individual stay away from another individual, location, or organization. Most often they prohibit *all* types of contact, including telephone calls, faxes, and letters as well as personal visits. Historically, people have been reluctant to obtain restraining orders for two major reasons: (1) They were thought to be ineffective, "not worth the paper they're written on"; and (2) they were thought to do little more than make the restrainee even more angry at the restrainer than he or she already was.

However, law enforcement agents have maintained that it is sometimes difficult, if not impossible, for them to carry out their responsibilities *without* a restraining order. An individual who is harassing another person or company isn't breaking the law unless the harassment consists of threats or other explicitly prohibited behaviors—unless there is a restraining order, in which case law enforcement agents can make an arrest for any kind of contact or communication.

Fear or reluctance to have one's name appear as the person requesting the restraining order is understandable, since it may enrage the restrainee even more. However, in many states this concern has been mitigated by the fact that it is now possible for an organization to obtain a restraining order against an individual. This allows the request to come from a department within a company (often the legal department or corporate counsel) as opposed to an individual employee or manager.

There are several philosophies on the proper use of restraining orders. One philosophy suggests that the court order should be sought only in those cases in which a terminated employee has actually committed "hands-on" violence. In other words, the individual has pushed, shoved, slapped, punched, and/or actually injured another person physically. The thinking here is that the offending person has shown through his or her behavior that he or she has both the desire and the capacity to be violent. It is further believed that when this desire and capacity are coupled with threats, the terminated employee should be seen as a potential risk for returning to the workplace and acting out again.

Another philosophy, which is much more conservative, suggests that the mere fact that a person is being terminated for breaching the company's policy on workplace violence is reason enough to seek a restraining order against that person. This way of thinking proposes that it is unreasonable and perhaps dangerous to wait until there is an incident of "hands-on" violence to seek the court's assistance.

The conservative approach has much merit. Companies should seek court intervention when an employee is terminated because (or mostly because) of acts or threats of violence. Speak to your corporate counsel and develop a strategy of seeking court support in cases of potential violence as an additional preventive tool.

If your violence prevention program includes seeking restraining orders against employees terminated for violent behavior, be sure to add the following steps to your termination procedures:

1. Immediately following the decision to terminate (but before the termination meeting or delivery of the termination letter), have your corporate counsel make application to the courts for a restraining order.

2. During the termination meeting inform the employee that you have sought a court order prohibiting contact. You do not want this to be a surprise when the employee is served notice.

3. If termination is done by letter and a follow-up call, include this information in both the letter and the phone conversation.

4. Inform receptionists, security guards, and other relevant employees (all those who are likely to see, hear, or receive communications from the terminated employee should he or she attempt to initiate contact) that there is a restraining order in effect against the terminated employee. Instruct these relevant employees that phone contacts, letters, and faxes from the terminated employee should

be directed to the contact person (preferably someone in security).

5. Inform relevant employees that they should call the police immediately if the terminated employee is seen entering or attempting to enter the workplace.

6. After calling the police, they should then contact in-house security.

7. Inform relevant employees that they are to complete steps 5 and 6 only *after* they have ensured their own safety (by exiting the building, retreating to a safe place, or whatever).

8. Even when no violence has occurred, any and all breaches of the court order must be reported to local law enforcement agencies and the courts.

Surveillance

There are times when it is a good idea to know where an individual is and what his or her activities include. Generally this is necessary in the most severe cases of criminal activity or potential violence. In these cases, the organization often finds that surveillance of an extremely hostile individual helps to keep bad intentions from becoming violent acts. Here are some guidelines for determining when such surveillance might be appropriate:

■ When an employee has made threats on the life of another—motive or intent

■ When the threatening individual has demonstrated the ability to carry out the threat (this will often involve a fascination with weapons)—means

■ When the threatening individual has left the organization but still has access to the premises (still has keys, for example)—opportunity

Should you ever find yourself with an employee (or former employee) who has the motive, means, and opportunity to commit seriously violent acts, you will want to contact your local law enforcement agency to get referrals to security organizations that can provide surveillance services. Also, be aware that some states have regulations governing how surveillance can be conducted. Your corporate counsel should be able to advise you regarding the regulations in your state.

Intervention Principles and Techniques

Too often friends, family members, co-workers, and supervisors are reluctant to confront a potentially violent person. They avoid intervening in the situation or otherwise getting involved despite obvious signs of potential danger. Perhaps they rationalize that any attempt at intervention will only set them up to be victimized. While this fear is understandable, it doesn't serve them well. For without appropriate intervention, the angry or disturbed person's negative feelings will only fester, and the inappropriate comments and behaviors that should serve as warning signs can escalate into violence.

The next question is, What exactly constitutes "appropriate intervention"? How does one get involved—with a potentially violent person, in a potentially violent situation—so as to calm the person down, diffuse the violent potential, and minimize or avoid further violence—or any violence at all?

There are some intervention principles and techniques that have proven to be more effective than others. We present them in this chapter, starting with some general principles of constructive confrontation and moving on to specific techniques for dealing with persons exhibiting the three stages of violent behavior as well as various warning signs.

Six Principles of Constructive Confrontation

Many people report that they "hate confrontation." And this is quite understandable. Constructive confrontation is one of the most difficult interpersonal skills to develop and master. It's often difficult to tell another person that his or her behavior is bothersome much less inappropriate or offensive, especially if your objective is to get the person to refrain from or change the behavior in question. And a potentially violent person is likely to react in a highly defensive manner—not listening to you, getting angry him- or herself, perhaps even turning the tables on you and criticizing or attacking you, verbally and/or physically.

However, we offer here six principles for constructively and effectively confronting potentially violent people and situations. These six principles, which are listed in the box on page 117, are appropriate guidelines for confronting all kinds of people in all kinds of situations, but they are especially useful whenever the person you're confronting or the situation you're trying to deal with involves the possibility of violence.

Some people equate confrontation with arguing. But they're really two different things. Certainly, attempts at confrontation can *devolve* into arguments, but we would not consider this *constructive* or *effective* confrontation (quite the opposite, in fact). Constructive confrontation involves addressing issues or prob-

---

Six Principles of Constructive Confrontation

1. Prepare

2. Address all the issues

3. Address only the issues

4. Offer options

5. Be flexible and accepting

6. Don't engage in verbal one-upmanship

---

lem areas that need to be addressed. It requires that the person raising the issues present his or her concerns in a concise, organized, and respectful manner. It also requires that the person raising the issues allow the confronted individual ample time to respond to them.

Prepare

Before you confront a potentially violent employee at work, you need to prepare for this discussion or meeting.

- You need to have documentation of the behavior that necessitates the meeting.

- You need to confer ahead of time with other relevant persons in your company: representatives from the security, human resources, and labor relations departments; members of the crisis management team; and maybe the administrator of your employee assistance program. The key here is that others must know in advance that you're going to confront this person, and why.

■ You also need to organize your own thoughts by focusing on what you want to accomplish in the meeting. Is this a disciplinary session, or is it merely an unofficial counseling session? The answer to this very basic question will strongly influence both the content and the tone of your remarks.

■ Finally, you need to consider and review your own attitudes and feelings toward the person you're about to speak with. If you dislike him or her, maybe you're not the best person to conduct this session. Perhaps your supervisor or someone from human resources or the crisis management team who has more positive (or at least neutral) feelings toward the person in question would be a better choice. And if you're afraid of the person who needs to be confronted, or have doubts about your ability to conduct the confrontation effectively, you might want to ask one of these other persons to sit in on the session with you, to back you up and help out as necessary.

Address All the Issues

Again, your preparation is the key here. Make sure that you have spoken to the individual's immediate supervisor, security, human resources, and any others who might have information regarding the inappropriate behavior you have to address. If it is possible to gather information about the person's private life that might be relevant, do so. Perhaps you should even write out a script of what the issues are and in what order you intend to address them. The point is that you want to make sure that you do not forget to address anything that is relevant to the issues at hand.

If you have prepared and organized your thoughts in this manner, you should not need to go back to the person later and bring up other issues that you have forgotten. To do so would make the person feel beaten up and picked on. Additionally, the goal is to correct an inappropriate behavior. Imagine if the person corrected his or her behavior only to be told that he or she was behaving inappropriately in another way as well. This would be insulting and demoralizing. This, of course, doesn't mean that if new issues come up they cannot be addressed; but try to make your meeting as complete as possible.

Address Only the Issues

One of the most destructive tactics is a "kitchen-sink" discussion. This is the type of discussion in which one brings up every issue or criticism one can think of. It tends to result from allowing tensions to accumulate and fester rather than dealing with each situation as it occurs. Very often the intended message (to stop behaving inappropriately) gets lost in all the comments about personality, likes, and dislikes.

If your discussion includes phrases such as "And another thing . . ."; "While we are here . . ."; "Since we have the time together . . ."; and/or "I've been meaning to tell you . . ." then you've probably been saving up your feedback and are on your way to a "kitchen-sink" discussion. Try to notice this and modify your approach.

Moreover, in addressing the potentially violent person, it is imperative that you address only the inappropriate *behaviors* and not cast aspersions on the person's character or morals. For example, "You are unreliable" is *not* acceptable feedback in this context, but "You have been late four of the last five workdays" is. The feedback must be specific and behavior-oriented.

Offer Options

You never want to make a person feel that his or her back is up against the wall, and that he or she has no way out of a bad situation—especially not someone who has exhibited violent behavior in the past. You always want to be able to present different options for how the person might correct the inappropriate behavior.

Your preparation will help with this. If you've prepared properly for the confrontation, you'll be able to describe to the person what resources are available to help him or her respond to the concerns you're raising. Can your company's employee assistance program help out in some way? Will the individual's health insurance carrier pay for some portion of the cost of counseling? If so, you want to be able to present these options during the course of your conversation.

Your general attitude and tone will also help convey your faith (or lack of it) in the person's ability to correct the inappropriate behavior. Phrases such as "What I'd like to see you do is . . ."; "This can be resolved by . . ."; and "What do you think we need to do to get you back on track here?" are all positive and constructive. They all indicate that, far from having given up on the employee, you're committed to working with him or her to resolve the problem and maintain the person as a productive member of your organization.

Be Flexible and Accepting

Assuming you've prepared properly, you'll have a clear agenda of the points you want to make during the confrontation. However, it is equally important that the employee be allowed to express his or her concerns and feelings as well. And some of those feelings may be negative ones—for example, anger, frustration, and resentment. Expressing such feelings verbally ("venting," in common parlance) is appropriate up to a point. However, if you or others in the meeting feel threatened or endangered in any way by how the person is responding, you'll need to put your agenda on hold temporarily and focus on regaining control of the present situation.

There are a number of methods of regaining control of the situation when the person you're confronting is losing control of his or her emotions. One way is to simply pause and ask the person if he or she would like a glass of water. Sometimes just giving the person a short break like this gives him or her a chance to calm down and regain control of his or her own emotions. You can also remind the person that the issues you're raising are professional, not personal; and you can reinforce through your own body language and tone that this is a professional conversation and that you expect professional conduct from the employee you're confronting.

Another good tactic to use when the person starts losing control is to break away from your agenda and simply acknowledge the person's feelings. Statements such as "You must be feeling a lot of pressure right now," or "You seem to be getting really angry with me" serve the same purpose as mirrors in a retail establishment: They reflect back to the person his or her own feelings and behavior, and help the person to modulate his or her behavior so that it remains acceptable and appropriate.

If none of these methods works, you may need to terminate the meeting, both to give the confronted employee a chance to cool off and to protect the safety of all those in attendance. If the employee is unable or unwilling to continue, you should indicate your wish to hold this meeting at a time when it can be more constructive, and simply reschedule it.

Don't Engage in Verbal One-Upmanship

Some people have a very hard time accepting criticism, no matter how appropriately worded or delivered. If you tell Kathy that she's been coming in late too often, she'll respond that others in her department take longer lunches than she does. Or if you tell Bob that his sexual joking is inappropriate, he'll say that everyone makes the same kind of jokes—even you. We call these kinds of responses "verbal one-upmanship."

Another possibility is that the employee may attempt (consciously or not) to engage you in an argument totally unrelated to the issue at hand. You may bring up some threats that Stuart has made recently, and he may launch into a long diatribe about the inadequate software support at your company, or the fact that the copy machines are always breaking down. This is simply a digression.

The thing to remember here is not to allow yourself to get caught up in such digressive arguments or battles of wits. Try to stay focused on the issues at hand. You want to be patient and allow the person to vent his or her feelings up to a point, but you don't want to let the person mount a verbal attack against you or lose sight of the main issues. If this begins to happen, you need to set limits: "I realize you're frustrated, Stuart, and that's fine, but I don't like the direction this conversation is taking. We need to focus right now on your recent threats—not on my behavior or on anyone else's behavior."

If setting limits in this way doesn't work, and the person persists in criticizing you or playing verbal one-upmanship in some other way, then you'll need to consider terminating the meeting and rescheduling it for a time when the person can focus on your agenda.

Techniques for Dealing with the Person Exhibiting Stage 1 Violent Behavior

Very often the individual exhibiting stage 1 violent behavior doesn't see his or her behavior as violent or even necessarily inappropriate. Colleagues, too, may view the person as "grouchy" or "hard to get along with" but not necessarily violent. However, stage 1 violent behavior is just that—the beginning of violence. And it is essential that you address the problem behaviors immediately, before they escalate to stage 2 or stage 3 behaviors. Indeed, how you respond to stage 1 violent behavior could very well determine whether or not the person goes on to commit actual physical violence. Simply put, the employee exhibiting stage 1 violent behavior needs to be made aware that such behaviors will *not* be tolerated.

Let's discuss an example showing the appropriate way to respond:

> Patrick, who works in the marketing department of a medical products company, has been extremely frustrated with the way things have been going at work lately. A few months ago, his company merged with a former competitor, and several new supervisors have been brought in to his department, bringing with them new philosophies, goals, and expectations. Several of these new supervisors happen to be Asian-American women, and Patrick, who is used to reporting to White men, seems to have a problem adjusting to this change (or rather, seems to be focusing on this fact as the symbol of all the changes he's having difficulty adjusting to). He has been overheard several times making crude comments about the sexual proclivities of these women, and has also used derogatory racial terms to refer to them.

Patrick is displaying stage 1 violent behavior. He's objectifying and dehumanizing others, and he's swearing excessively and using sexually explicit and otherwise inappropriate language. There's also been a decline in his productivity of late, which you'll recall is a warning sign.

It could be that this employee is just blowing off steam, and that as soon as he adjusts to the various changes his company is going through, he'll settle down and be fine. Then again, it's equally possible that this could be the beginning of an escalation toward even greater violence. Since there's no way to know or determine which of these explanations is more true, it's appropriate to respond as if this is the beginning of even greater violence.

To begin with, Patrick's supervisor should address his recent decline in productivity:

Manager: Good morning, Patrick. Recently I've noticed that your productivity seems to have gone down. This seems strange to me, since you have always been one of the top performers around here. Is something going on that I can help you with?

Employee: Well, I am kind of frustrated.

Manager: I'm willing to listen if you're willing to share your frustrations with me.

Employee: It's just all these changes lately; they're really starting to get to me. . . .

After completing the discussion about Patrick's frustrations, his supervisor should then address the inappropriateness of the comments he's been overheard making lately:

Manager: Now that we have discussed your frustrations, I have some concerns of my own. I know that you are familiar with our workplace violence policy; have you reread it lately?

Employee: No, but who's been violent?

Manager: Well, Patrick, I suggest you read it again. Here's a copy. It states clearly that inflammatory language such as ethnic slurs and swearing is a form of violence. In addition, sexually inappropriate language creates a hostile work environment and is therefore unacceptable.

Employee: I was just blowing off steam. I didn't intend to hurt anybody.

Manager: I'm glad to hear that, but you also need to remember that aggressive language is a form of violence and will be treated as such. I would like to consider this meeting the last time I'll need to remind you about your language. Are we in agreement?

Employee: Okay, sure.

Note that the supervisor listened to Patrick and accepted his frustrations. Moreover (presumably), the supervisor offered some suggestions for how Patrick might better deal with his frustrations and improve his performance while avoiding making inappropriate comments at work. In addition, the supervisor should document this discussion and should follow up with Patrick in a week or so to check that the strategies they developed and agreed on for improving his performance and behavior have been successful.

It's important to stress that Patrick's supervisor isn't the only person in this scenario responsible for dealing with his violent behavior. *Everyone* in the workplace has a responsibility to ensure that the working environment remains safe. In this example, Patrick's colleagues made note of his inappropriate comments and reported them to his supervisor (or perhaps to their own supervisor). Nor should these colleagues be considered "tattletales" or "informers" in a pejorative sense, for their actions constitute an important component in an effective response to stage 1 violent behavior.

Techniques for Dealing with the Person Exhibiting Stage 2 Violent Behavior

Stage 2 violent behavior represents an escalation from stage 1, and thus should cause some concern. Stage 2 can be considered the "bridge" from angry thoughts to angry actions. The danger with stage 2 violent behavior is that it's just a step away from actual physical violence. Recall that two of the most common characteristic stage 2 behaviors are blaming others and making verbal threats. Be on the lookout for those two behaviors as you consider the following example:

> Diane has worked for a leading clothing manufacturing company for the last twelve years. During that time she has always been a line employee, actually cutting the cloth or working the sewing machines

to assemble the finished items. She has taken the test to be a supervisor seven times, including just a couple of weeks ago, but has failed it each time. She has seen many, many employees who started with the company *after* she did, promoted ahead of her.

Since Diane found out a couple of weeks ago that she failed the test yet again, she has expressed a lot of anger and frustration over what she perceives as a biased and unfair promotion process. (Although the majority of line employees are female, the majority of supervisors are male.) One day she yelled at several men who did pass the supervisor's test, calling them "male-chauvinist pigs." Diane's supervisor spoke to her about this incident, and it seemed that her anger was, and would continue to be, under control. However, today she came in twenty minutes late and became indignant when one of the recently promoted supervisors asked her for an explanation. She told this person not to "mess" with her today, and made a veiled reference to feeling "real postal whenever I think about those test results." She also said that she "hates this goddamn place."

Diane has demonstrated both stage 1 and stage 2 violent behaviors. Not only has she been objectifying others, swearing, and abusing others verbally; she's also holding others responsible for her failure to get promoted and has made an indirect verbal threat to come in with a gun and start shooting. We'll assume that her supervisor responded correctly when he spoke to her about her inappropriate language; however, her violent behavior has escalated nonetheless. Now a more vigorous response is called for.

Obviously, Diane's supervisor needs to meet with her and speak to her again. Before doing so, however, the supervisor should first do the following:

- Alert security that a threat has been made.
- Review the company's guidelines and stipulations regarding suspensions.

- Review Diane's work history and performance appraisals for indications of past problems.

- Contact the company's crisis management team for help planning the meeting with Diane.

- Develop an agenda for the meeting. This agenda should include suspending her or placing her on leave until a fitness-for-duty evaluation has been completed and she has been cleared.

- Schedule the meeting with Diane. Inform in-house security (or another colleague, if there is no in-house security at the company) of where and when the meeting is scheduled. Have someone remain nearby during the meeting in case assistance is required.

- Arrange the furniture in the office in such a manner that the supervisor is sitting closer to the door than Diane, just in case escape becomes necessary. If this is not possible, arrange to meet in a conference room.

During the meeting with Diane, the supervisor should do the following:

- Explain the reason for this meeting. Be specific; detail the troubling behaviors.

- Allow Diane every opportunity to present her side of the story.

- Ask her if there is anything the company can do to help her with her stress.

- Make referrals and offer options.

- Remind her of the company's policy on violence, which includes threats.

- Explain that it is management's responsibility to provide for her safety and the safety of other employees, and therefore she is being suspended until she is cleared for further work.

After the meeting with Diane, the supervisor should do the following:

■ Immediately document the conversation. Make certain that the members of the crisis management team receive the report.

■ Have in-house security (or other appropriate administrators) escort Diane from the premises.

■ Have a human resources manager contact Diane to arrange for a fitness-for-duty evaluation.

Techniques for Dealing with the Person Exhibiting Stage 3 Violent Behavior

While stage 1 and stage 2 behaviors are preliminary forms of violence, the most severe forms of violence are the behaviors we classify as stage 3: actual physical confrontations, displaying weapons, committing assault, and so on. As we explained in chapter 5, attempting to defuse stage 3 violent behavior is ill-advised, for the person you're dealing with is not likely to respond to reason. Supervisors and managers (and, indeed, all responsible persons) have three responsibilities when they encounter stage 3 violent behavior:

1. Get out of harm's way.

2. Warn others.

3. Contact the authorities.

Getting Out of Harm's Way

Often when we tell people that their first obligation is to remove themselves from harm, their response is that they know that already, and that that would be their instinctive reaction anyway—to get out of there as quickly as possible. The fact is, though, that this isn't what most people do. Many people like to watch the violent scene unfolding in front of them. (In fact, when police officers are trying to apprehend a person wielding a gun, one of their biggest concerns is crowd control—trying to keep onlookers at a safe distance.) Others, especially men, have been socialized to believe that it's cowardly to flee, and unmanly even to be afraid in the face of violence.

However, unless you have specialized training in dealing with the most extreme forms of violent behavior, you're far better off getting away from the scene, or protecting yourself in whatever way possible, and calling for professional help if you can. Getting out of harm's way may involve leaving the floor or building or even hiding under a desk. Only you can decide what's safest under the circumstances.

Warning Others

While each of us is primarily responsible for our own safety, we also have a moral obligation to warn other potential victims of the danger at hand. This obligation does *not* require you to put your own safety at risk. What it *does* require is that as you yourself are getting out of harm's way, you alert others whom you encounter to do the same—especially those who may be unwittingly walking into the line of fire.

Contacting the Authorities

Once you've gotten yourself out of harm's way and warned others of the danger at hand, you must contact the appropriate authorities so that they can intervene appropriately. The appropriate authorities may be in-house security or local law enforcement agencies. There's a tendency to think that someone has already made the call, so you don't need to. This is a mistake. Let the authorities tell you that they are already aware of the situation, but don't make that assumption yourself.

Techniques for Dealing with the Warning Signs of Violent Behavior

The nine warning signs of violent behavior, which are thoroughly described in chapter 3, pose some unique challenges. All of them are associated with an increased risk for violent behavior, but none of them is a guarantee or absolute predictor that the person will become violent. For example, decreased or inconsistent productivity could be the result of health problems and have no connection to violence whatsoever. And although we all experience severe stress at different times in our lives, most of us manage to deal with it without resorting to violent outbursts. Sometimes a bad hair day is just a bad hair day; yet sometimes it's just the tip of the iceberg of problems underneath the surface. That's why the warning signs need to be investigated—not in the sense of a security or police investigation necessarily, but in the sense of trying to determine whether the warning sign is cause for further alarm.

One thing to keep in mind is that the truly violent person rarely exhibits only one warning sign or indicator of violent potential. A fascination with weapons, on its own, probably *isn't* cause for concern. But when the individual also has a substance abuse problem, a violent history, and/or a tendency to swear excessively and argue frequently, then that *combination* of warning signs and stage 1 violent behaviors *is* cause for alarm. Consider the following example:

> Kevin, who drives a forklift for a construction company, has a gun collection; he talks about it with his co-workers freely and often. Kevin is also a reliable worker who gets along well with his peers. He's been with the company for eleven years. He's married and has two children: He speaks with pride of their activities and accomplishments, and likes to show off pictures of his family. Other than his fascination with weapons, Kevin has exhibited no other warning sign of

violent behavior. Still, just to be on the safe side, his supervisor decides to speak with him, to try to determine the level of risk that Kevin may pose. Their conversation goes as follows:

Manager: Morning, Kevin. How are you?

Employee: Good. How about you?

Manager: I am good, Kevin, but I would like to touch base with you about something.

Employee: What's up?

Manager: I have overheard you speak about your guns a lot recently.

Employee: Yeah, my father died last year and left me his gun collection. I was never really into guns or shooting until he left them to me. Now I get some pleasure out of owning something that was so important to him. It's like we're sharing a hobby even though he's no longer here.

Manager: I didn't know about your father. I'm sorry to hear he died. But, I have to ask you, do you ever bring any of these guns to work?

Employee: No. I keep them locked up in my father's gun vault. I think they may be worth some money.

Manager: I'm happy for you, Kevin. I had to ask, because of our policy against weapons at work.

Employee: No problem.

In this example it's clear that Kevin's interest in guns (and ownership of guns) does *not* pose an increased risk for violence in the workplace. He's a good worker, with no history of problems or conflicts at his company. He obviously cares a great deal about his family, and it's unlikely he would do anything to jeopardize their stability. He's in control of his emotions and his life; he's made no threats to anyone, and he doesn't appear to have any simmering anger. Conclusion: No further action is necessary. Even though there's no apparent threat here, the supervisor would need to document the conversation he or she had with Kevin about his guns—but merely as a record that the conversation took place and that the warning sign was determined *not* to be a cause for alarm.

Now let's consider a different example:

Timothy, who drives a forklift for the same construction company, also has some guns, and also talks about them freely and often. Timothy is not married; he had a stormy, on-and-off relationship with a girlfriend for a while, but as far as his co-workers know, that's over now. Timothy has had a few disagreements with his co-workers in the last several months. None of these disagreements was considered to be major, but there was some yelling and cursing involved, and a couple of times Timothy stormed away muttering what may have been threats under his breath. Somebody asked him later what it was he'd said, and he made some vague comment about "seeking justice." He hasn't directly threatened anyone, but some of his co-workers have started to avoid him nonetheless.

His supervisor decides to speak with him, both about his gun collection in particular and about this more general pattern of threatening behavior. In preparing for the meeting, the supervisor checks Timothy's personnel records and finds that in the past nine months, he's had an unusually high number of sick days, has been warned and disciplined several times for being late, and has also been warned for insubordination (he refused to take an assignment and got into an argument with a supervisor over it). Their conversation goes something like this:

Manager: Good morning, Timothy.

Employee: Yeah?

Manager: How're you doing?

Employee: What do you need?

Manager: I have a few concerns I want to speak to you about.

Employee: Now what?

Manager: I'm concerned, Timothy, because recently you haven't been as reliable in your work as you used to be. There've been some complaints that you've been getting into a lot of arguments lately. Also, I've heard you talking a lot about guns. Boy, those two things together can be real scary. Is something going on that I can help you with?

Employee: Yeah, well, people have been giving me a real hard time lately. And I just wanted them to know that I will only take it for so long.

Manager: You will only take what for so long?

Employee: I will only take the crap I get from these pea brains around here for so long.

Manager: You seem pretty upset about something. With all your talk about guns, I'm wondering if you're thinking about hurting someone?

Employee: Not at the moment, but you never know what will happen when people push you hard enough.

Is there a problem here? Most definitely. Timothy's responses during this conversation, in combination with his recent behavior at work, spell trouble. In this case, the employee's fascination with (and ownership of) guns wasn't the only factor that seemed to indicate violent potential; in fact, there are a whole slew of others: his argumentativeness and frequent swearing, his increasing social isolation, and his declining performance on the job. This time the supervisor's investigation uncovered genuine potential for violence. Now it's time for the supervisor to develop and implement a plan for dealing with that violent potential—and it had better include removing Timothy from the workplace, at least temporarily, to protect everyone's safety.

To summarize, then, when a supervisor observes or is made aware of one or more of the warning signs of violent behavior, he or she should take the following steps:

- Review the employee's work history with the company. Look for a record of other warning signs or stage 1 violent behaviors.

- Inform the crisis management team of the concerns about the warning sign(s). If the company doesn't have a crisis management team, inform security and human resources of these concerns.

- Develop a plan before speaking with the employee. This plan should include what action to take in the event that the employee poses a violent threat (for example, suspension or termination).

- Schedule a meeting with the individual displaying the warning sign(s). If the threat of violence appears to be significant and immediate, request that security or some other appropriate person sit in on the meeting.

- Present only factual information during the meeting.

- Allow plenty of time for the individual to respond to the concerns. Listen carefully to what he or she has to say.

- In the event of feeling threatened or endangered in any way during the meeting, terminate it at once.

Case Studies and Assessment

This section will help you to assess your organization's preparedness to deal with potential and actual workplace violence. It begins with a chapter describing some of the worst practices for dealing with workplace violence, followed by a chapter describing some of the best practices, and closes with a chapter containing eight questionnaires, or self-tests, to help you assess your organization's "violence quotient." Use this section as a step-by-step guide for implementing or improving your company's violence prevention and intervention program.

chapter 8

Worst Practices for Dealing with Workplace Violence

This chapter will consider several real-life organizations and their practices for dealing with workplace violence. These are examples of things you do *not* want to see or do in your organization. While we know that no one can make another person act out violently, we also know that when certain conditions exist, the potential for violence increases. Be sure that these conditions do *not* exist in your company. If they do, address them immediately! These cases are real. The names of the organizations and the individuals involved have been changed to protect their identity. In some cases, the geographical location or type of industry has been changed as well. This was done because some of the companies might have been identifiable based solely on what they do. But the relevant facts regarding violent individuals and incidents—and how the companies responded to them—have not been altered or made up.

Worst Practices Example #1

The Uninformed Dictator

Mesa is a small consulting firm in southern California. Their clientele ranges from medium to large companies, and these companies usually seek out Mesa's help in dealing with personnel matters. Mesa employs about twenty full-time workers. Up until recently, Mesa was run by its board of directors. There was a president at the helm, but he was president by title only, and lacked even the most rudimentary management skills. In fact, the employees long ago learned to disregard anything he said because of his gross incompetence and inability to lead. Finally, though, the board of directors decided that it was time to bring in an effective president to manage the company.

The board selected John to be the new president. He had a lot of management experience and was supposed to be a quick study. On his first day at Mesa, he told the two senior professionals there that they had "failed miserably," and that he was hired to "clean up the mess" they had made. He also informed them that "from today forward, it will be my way or the highway around here." He then told the only two clerical workers that there would be some staffing reductions, and that one, and possibly both, of them "were history."

Even though generating a steady flow of revenue had never been a problem before (the company was very busy with its clients), it soon became one. As each of the workers at the company began to wonder when the hatchet would fall, they began to spend their days looking at their options outside of Mesa. This caused a drop in productivity, billings, and revenue. The drop in revenue caused John to worry about the board's impression of him—which then caused him to be even more cost-conscious and difficult to deal with.

When faced with the resentment of the workers, John began to use their pay—specifically, the threat of withholding it—as a tool of manipulation. Those workers who went along with John got paid. Those who challenged him (even if they were right) did not. Within six months of John's arrival, six employees had resigned to work elsewhere. These were people who decided that it was better to leave than to stay and be browbeaten and manipulated.

When the board expressed concern about the flight of the company's workers, John was able to explain it away by saying that he had been trying to cut expenses and that the people who had left were expendable. However, several workers who also wanted to leave could not, as they had not received any offers outside the company. Those individuals stayed and allowed their anger and resentment toward John—and the company—to fester and grow. One of those workers who stayed was Fred.

Fred was 54 years old, and married with four children. His performance at Mesa before John's arrival had been marginal at best. He usually tried to find ways to avoid doing any work, and always had an excuse for not being able to take on a new client. Most people in the company believed that Fred was simply waiting for the company to go public so that he could sell the stock he had from the employee stock purchase program. The company probably should have let him go years ago.

Once John arrived and instituted his bullying and manipulative tactics, Fred's behavior became more and more underhanded. He often created a family crisis so that he could "work" from home, though it was doubtful that he even tried to get anything done on those days. Often he manipulated other, less-senior workers into doing his work for him. However, Fred was a "yes-man" to John. He was also very good friends with a board member. This board member gave John the clear message that Fred was "protected." So Fred stayed despite his limited productivity.

The atmosphere and prevailing attitude at Mesa became one of "me first." Most of the remaining employees sought to do only the minimum that was required of them; their main objective seemed to be staying out of John's way. The form of violence perpetrated by nearly all of the remaining workers was *sabotage*—in small ways at first; then in increasingly harmful ways. The infighting became incredible. Most of the employees attempted to portray themselves to John as agreeing with his direction and being on his side. But behind his back, they all griped about what a poor leader they thought he was. The sabotage and infighting caused Mesa to lose more than one client, and because John lacked the trust and genuine support of his employees, he didn't have a clue as to what was actually going on.

Lesson

Deal with problems when they occur.

What forms of violence did you detect in the above scenario? What could have been done to prevent further acts of aggression at Mesa?

Let's first talk about Fred. We can tell a lot about this company just from the fact that Fred was allowed to survive there. If the description of Fred's performance as "marginal at best" is accurate, then the company should have taken steps to get him to improve his performance long before John came aboard. Too often, organizations allow individuals to remain at a subpar performance level. Often, as in the above case, it is easier to just ignore the problem rather than deal with it. In these cases we tell ourselves, "Well, this is all we're going to get from Fred. We might as well get used to it." However, this rationalization is fair neither to Fred nor to his co-workers. Often, when we talk to a nonperforming employee, that person will tell us that he or she had no idea that the company was unhappy with his or her performance. Admittedly, this is sometimes an excuse or an outright lie. There are times when employees are notified of their shortcomings and opt not to do anything about it, hoping that the pressure to improve will simply go away. More commonly, though, no one ever bothers to give accurate feedback to the nonperforming (or underperforming) employee. The management at Mesa should have spoken to Fred, given him explicit instructions and goals for improving his performance, and indicated a time frame for making the necessary adjustments.

The next problem at Mesa was John, the new president. Why didn't anyone on the board notice or care that within six months of his arrival many of the professionals at Mesa had resigned? When revenue flow became a problem, for the first time ever in the company's history, this too should have been a red flag. John's leadership style, which is still very much present in corporate America, neither appreciates nor tolerates either differences of opinion or challenges from subordinates. This style involves methods of manipulation that are sometimes illegal and always cause for resentment. John's act of paying only those employees who agreed with him is clearly against the law. Even if it were not illegal, however, it certainly wouldn't result in the employees' having the company's best interests in mind. Employees in this type of company concern themselves only with "what is good for me." Manipulation and sabotage become normal, everyday activities.

Instead of withholding pay in an attempt to motivate improved productivity, John should have evaluated every employee's performance in a more appropriate manner. If there were lapses or incompetence, he should have informed the employee of his expectations. If these expectations weren't met, he should have disciplined and/or terminated the employee. At no time and in no case should an employee's wages or salary be withheld to gain compliance. (This, of course, does not include those times when an employee is placed on formal suspension and loss of pay is part of that suspension.)

Another problem at Mesa was the employees themselves. If we accept the premise that everyone in the workplace has a responsi-

bility to maintain a violence-free work environment, then no violent behavior can be excused, even in circumstances in which an
individual has clearly been wronged. The employees at Mesa had a
responsibility to act within the system to regain their rights. While
the behavior of John and Fred was inexcusable, so too was the
sabotage committed by other employees. Instead of sabotaging the
company (and each other), they should have gone to John and
demanded their salaries, gone to the board of directors to report
John's illegal behavior, and/or gone to the labor board to report
the illegal acts taking place at their company. The employee's interest is always better served when he or she acts with integrity.
When a situation is out of control, the employee should do what
he or she can to improve it—or leave the situation entirely.
(Indeed, those workers who resigned at least acted with integrity.)

Finally, the board member who explicitly or implicitly protected
Fred is at fault here as well. When an organization allows a nonperforming individual to thrive because of a "special relationship," it's
giving a clear message to other employees that they are not valued.
And organizations that don't value each employee set themselves
up for growing resentment and potential violence.

Worst Practices Example #2
Boys Will Be Boys

Burns is a mid-Atlantic steel company. One of the largest manufacturing companies on the East Coast, Burns employs about
eleven hundred employees. Most of these employees are males
between the ages of 19 and 45. With all the testosterone flow-
ing in their veins, the atmosphere can get very boisterous at
times. Name-calling and roughhousing are quite common at
the plant. Fistfights are also a regular occurrence. Most often
these fistfights are seen as "just the boys mixing it up," and are
not taken seriously.

Mike and Ray have worked for the company for eight and ten
years, respectively. They don't like each other. Mike is kind of

a loudmouth and brags a lot. Ray is somewhat reserved, but considers himself to be a lady's man. They are both shift supervisors. Mike supervises the second shift, which works from 3:00 P.M. until 11:00 P.M. Ray supervises the third shift, which works from 11:00 P.M. until 7:00 A.M. They rarely actually see each other, but when they do, it's never pleasant. One or the other always has a wisecrack or insult for the other.

Most recently, Ray has been complaining about how messy Mike and his crew leave the workstation after their shift. Mike's response is that the problem is Ray's and he couldn't care less about it. On one Thursday morning at about 1:30 A.M., Ray phones Mike at home to complain about the sloppy conditions. Mike, who is home with his wife and about to go to bed, hangs up on Ray. But Ray phones back and threatens Mike, saying, "I'll kick your ass if you ever hang up the phone on me again." Mike then says, "You have an ass-whipping coming for phoning me at home in the first place. I'll see you in the morning." And he hangs up again.

The next morning, Mike gets to the plant at the end of the third shift, looking for Ray. Once he spots him, he runs up and begins punching Ray. Caught off guard, Ray immediately falls to the floor, where Mike continues to pound him in the face. When Ray's face is bloodied and bruised, co-workers standing nearby finally try to pull Mike off him. Mike gets in one last kick to Ray's groin before allowing the co-workers to pull him off.

Ray refuses assistance as he picks himself up off the floor. He yells to Mike, who is now walking away laughing with friends, "We aren't done yet. You'll get yours." Mike ignores Ray. Ray makes his way back to the locker room. He retrieves a box cutter (a small knife used to open boxes) from his locker and seeks out Mike. He finds him standing with some friends. Before Mike even notices Ray, Ray swipes at him with the box cutter, stabbing him in the abdomen. There is blood everywhere. Ray leaves the scene as some co-workers tend to Mike and call for an ambulance. Mike is taken to the local hospital, where his wound (which is relatively minor, as it turns out) is stitched up and he is then released. The police arrest Ray at his home. He is booked on charges of assault with a deadly weapon and released on bond.

The management of Burns sends a message to Ray explaining that he should consider himself suspended until further notice. He is told not to come into work nor to contact the company in any way. Mike, on the other hand, is allowed to use some of his sick leave while he recovers from his wound. He is told that he can come back to work as soon as his doctor okays it. Within twenty-four hours, the administration decides to terminate Ray. He is sent a registered letter informing him of this decision. After three days, Mike returns to work.

Lesson

Have a workplace violence policy and a plan for dealing with violators.

There are many problems at the Burns plant. To begin with, such violent behaviors as name-calling, roughhousing, and fistfights are all commonplace. First and foremost, Burns should have a workplace violence policy forbidding all these behaviors. The workers at the plant should be expected to treat each other in a dignified and respectful manner at all times. The company's policies and procedures manual must forbid fighting, for any reason, and must impose strict consequences for breaking this rule.

The next area of concern is that co-workers would stand by and watch while two workers were fighting. Why didn't someone call for security or a supervisor? Why didn't the onlookers themselves try to break up the fight sooner? This lack of response reflects a culture or an atmosphere that allows—perhaps even encourages—settling conflicts physically. Additionally, if Ray had a legitimate gripe with Mike, he should have known that the appropriate thing to do would have been to go to his supervisor. Instead, Ray phoned Mike at home. Similarly, if these calls from Ray bothered Mike, his response should have been to report the incident to a supervisor. Instead Mike chose to settle the dispute by attacking Ray physically. These actions on both their parts suggest that the administration of the company had very little control over its workers. Is it possible that the company's position on such personnel conflicts was, "We are only here to make money. Don't bother us with these personnel concerns"?

Finally, the company chose to terminate Ray. Appropriate enough—but why not Mike as well? Wasn't Mike as much at fault as Ray in this scenario? After all, Mike initiated the physical confrontation; he threw the first punch. It would perhaps be most appropriate to terminate both of these men from the company. And to make matters worse, both of them were supervisors in the organization. It doesn't speak well for the leadership of the company when those who have been selected to monitor and evaluate others are prone to fighting themselves.

Worst Practices Example #3

A Screen with a Big Hole in It

Sci-fi, Inc., is an international high-tech company. Their business is wide-ranging but focuses primarily on finding new ways to use emerging technologies. They are involved in everything from the development of new types of plastics to finding new sources of energy. And they have offices in every region of the United States and in many foreign countries also.

Sci-fi has every conceivable security plan in place for screening applicants, including very complete background checks, psychological assessments, several personal interviews, and even polygraph interviews. They also have a very thorough workplace violence policy and a crisis management team. (Sci-fi also employs its own security force, many of whom are well trained and armed.)

Because Sci-fi's screening process can take as long as thirteen months to complete, there have been times when the company has been unable to make a job offer until after the applicant has already accepted another position elsewhere. This usually happens when the applicant is between jobs and doesn't want to wait any longer for Sci-fi to complete its screening process.

Dave is a 33-year-old computer security specialist. He spent four years in the military, where he received some training in technology security. His areas of specialty are hardware, software, and keeping information from being misused or stolen. When he applied for a position at Sci-fi, given his experience and obvious intelligence Sci-fi was thrilled at the prospect of bringing him on board. He quickly and completely filled out all the application documents, though he seemed to have a somewhat difficult time listing personal references.

The job Dave applied for required a special security clearance, and he was informed that this process could take some time. In fact, he was told, it could take up to a year. However, not wanting to lose such a bright young prospect, Sci-fi allowed Dave to begin working as soon as his education and military record were confirmed, which happened almost right away. The deal was to allow Dave to work in an area that required a lower-level security clearance than the job he had applied for until his high-level clearance came through.

After nine months with the company, Dave had become virtually indispensable. He was quick and eager to learn, and always willing to fill in for someone who was sick or otherwise unavailable. After ten months with the company, Dave was allowed to work in the high-clearance position he had originally applied for. After all, Sci-fi reasoned, it was just a matter of time before his security clearance would come through.

After having been with the company about one and a half years, Dave seemed to be working out fairly well. It turned out that he didn't know as much about the field as he had professed, but he learned quickly. His supervisors did have a few problems with Dave, however: They were frustrated at having to teach him things that he was supposed to know already; and once instructed, Dave became the self-proclaimed expert. As one supervisor put it, "I'll teach the guy something on Friday, and on Monday he'll tell me how I'm doing it wrong." There were several low-level confrontations on the subject of expertise between Dave and his supervisors. Another supervisor commented, "Dave takes instruction well . . . the first time. After that, he doesn't want to hear it because he thinks he knows it all already."

On one occasion, in an attempt to demonstrate that security at Sci-fi was weak, Dave brought a gun to work in his briefcase. Upon passing the security checkpoint, he removed the gun from his briefcase and, waving it in the air to prove his point, yelled at the guards, "You see, you see, I told you guys you had it all wrong!" Not only did this incident scare many of the employees who happened to be coming into work at the time, but it also caused a lot of embarrassment to the security department that Dave worked for. When Dave's supervisor sat him down and explained that this antic was not the appropriate way to improve security, Dave lost his temper. "You're just mad because you have egg on your face," he yelled at his boss. "No," said the supervisor, "We have some areas that we need to improve on, but why would you want all the employees, contractors, and vendors who happened to witness this to know that they could get a gun in here if they really wanted to?" But Dave refused to acknowledge that he had done anything wrong. A report about the incident was placed in his file, but otherwise the incident was basically forgotten.

However, shortly after this gun-waving episode, Dave's supervisor happened to mention to the background investigator that Dave still had not received his security clearance. The investigator, with a sheepish look, responded that there was a problem with the background check. While he couldn't be specific, the investigator said that there were some things in Dave's application that didn't meet the standard for the type of clearance he sought. "How long have you known this?" said the supervisor. The investigator replied that he had become aware of the problem about four months ago. "Why didn't you let me know?" said the supervisor. The investigator replied, "It's pretty routine that when someone doesn't pass, we try to find out if it's because of blanks on the application or a real security concern. Anyway, I was just trying to help you out. I was trying to get the guy cleared since you'd already approved him to start working in the high-clearance area."

So began a long battle for the company. Sci-fi immediately sought to dismiss Dave because he couldn't obtain the security clearance needed to perform his duties. Dave responded by threatening to file a wrongful termination suit. His position was that a security clearance must not be necessary since he had already been working at the company for two years without one. During the dispute, Dave made several remarks that amounted to threats on the lives of certain Sci-fi executives should he lose his job. Sci-fi then tried to fire Dave because such threats were explicitly forbidden by the company's workplace violence policy. Dave countered that this attempt to terminate him was retaliatory in nature. He made it clear that his intent was to keep his job or "fight this thing for as long as I have to."

Sci-fi did fire Dave. And he did file a wrongful termination suit, as he had promised. We never heard how the lawsuit was resolved, or if it's still pending.

Lesson

Always follow your company's screening procedures, to the letter.

As we have discussed earlier in this book, having a workplace violence policy that no one is aware of or adheres to is useless.

Additionally, having a full-blown violence prevention program that is either ignored or undercut defeats its purpose. Many organizations have the necessary policies and procedures in place to prevent workplace violence, but fail to follow or use them on a consistent basis. (To give a few other examples, we have visited organizations that have code-key entry into the parking lots, but employees defeat the system by placing cinder blocks on the gate to prevent its closing. This is often done to accommodate those employees who are running late and don't want to take the time to punch in the code. Likewise, many companies deny access to their buildings to all except those who have been issued card-keys. Yet this system is often defeated by the individual who goes out for a smoke but doesn't bring his or her keys, so the person props the door open instead.)

Sci-fi's problems in the case we just read are threefold. First, there seems to be some thinking, on the part of at least some employees, that the company goes overboard in its security measures. Obviously, the supervisor in the scenario believed that he was a better judge of who should be employed by the company than the investigators and the system designed to keep trouble out. Sci-fi needs to educate all its employees on the reasons for security precautions, making sure everyone understands that the screening of applicants and other security measures are in place not just to protect the company's assets, but to protect people as well. Moreover, security personnel should be people-friendly, to avoid the perception that they are just "the people who hassle me when I come in to work every day." In addition, those responsible for recruiting or screening applicants should make very clear to them the time frame involved. Recruiters should also take note of a candidate's ability to earn a living during the lengthy screening process. This could perhaps reduce anxiety about the possibility of losing a "great prospect" because he or she had to take another position in order to support him- or herself. Finally, investigators should make a point of informing each candidate and hiring supervisor of exactly where the investigators are in the screening process. For example, "We have completed the reference check, and so far so good. The next phase is the personal interview."

The second area of concern for Sci-fi is the supervisor who decided to allow Dave to work in a high-security position before he received clearance. It was a bad idea to allow Dave to work at all before the screening process was complete. It was a worse idea to allow Dave to begin working in a high-security position. Perhaps the supervisor was feeling pressure to get more work done, and lacked sufficient personnel. If that's the case, though, this supervisor should have gone to his supervisor and explained the situation. Under no circumstances should an individual undercut the security measures an organization has set up to protect its people and assets.

Finally, there's the investigator. Four months before his discussion with the supervisor, he was aware that there was a problem with Dave's application for security clearance. Yet he told no one, and sought instead to clear the guy. This compounding of the problem is also very common in organizations. Someone realizes that there is a problem, but instead of communicating with others about it and dealing with it appropriately, the person attempts to cover it up and make it all right. Could a legal battle have been avoided if the investigator had immediately conveyed the information about Dave's being denied clearance? We'll never know. We can say, though, that the investigator's attempt to cover up a bad decision (or a series of bad decisions) on the part of the supervisor served only to compound the company's problems in this scenario.

9

Best Practices
for Dealing with
Workplace Violence

There are organizations that have been proactive in their fight against workplace violence. These companies, some public and others private, have worked hard to establish and maintain violence-free work environments. The examples described in this chapter are actual companies that have done a great deal to prepare for the worst. The names of companies and individuals have been changed to protect their privacy.

Best Practices Example #1
Nipping a Problem in the Bud

California Electronics Company (CEC) is a large, international computer-chip manufacturer that has developed a strict policy prohibiting workplace violence. Its policy spells out exactly what violence is and what the consequences are for breaching the policy. CEC has also implemented a campaign to make certain that all employees are aware of the policy. When a new employee is hired, that individual is required to read the policy and sign a statement confirming that he or she has read it and understands it.

CEC employs many engineers and computer specialists. These professionals aren't necessarily any more violent than any other workers. However, these types of professionals sometimes prefer—and are better at—dealing with computers or tasks than dealing with people. This personality trait sometimes causes co-workers to perceive them as "cold," "distant," or "dangerous." CEC has known for years that many of the complaints about such professionals are without merit. Nonetheless, whenever a complaint comes in, it is investigated.

Bill is a 42-year-old computer specialist at CEC. He has been described as "very bright," but also "kind of strange." He has worked at CEC for nine years, and his performance there has been outstanding. He has, however, been spoken to about his tendency to show up for work twenty to thirty minutes late. Bill explained that sometimes he starts working on his computer at home in the early morning and loses track of time. However, when his supervisor reiterated the business need for all employees to be at the office during normal working hours, Bill did agree to make every effort to get to work on time, and there has been no further problem with Bill and tardiness.

Stacey works in the same department as Bill. She has had few conversations with him and reports that he "likes to work and doesn't like to talk to anyone." On one occasion when Stacey asked Bill for some assistance in performing a task, Bill "snapped" at her. Stacey says that he told her to "leave me the hell alone." Knowing the company's policy on aggressive language, Stacey reported this incident to the human resources department. Paul, an HR representative, interviewed Stacey to get all the details. Paul then interviewed Bill's supervisor to get a feel for Bill's performance. The supervisor mentioned that Bill had been showing up late, but reported that the situation had been resolved and that there were no further problems. After reviewing Bill's files, Paul scheduled a meeting with him. The meeting took place in a private conference room, to lessen the possibility of embarrassing Bill. Paul did not anticipate encountering any problems, but he informed security of the meeting time and date anyway, in keeping with the company's violence prevention plan.

At the meeting, Paul greeted Bill and offered him coffee. Once seated, Bill expressed concern at being asked to meet with an HR representative. Paul attempted to assure Bill that the meeting would not be as painful as he might have imagined. Paul stated that he had received reports that Bill had cursed at a co-worker and that the co-worker was now afraid of Bill. Paul asked Bill if he recalled the incident. Bill did. Paul then asked Bill to explain the circumstances. Bill looked apologetic and explained that he sometimes gets so wrapped up in a project that any disturbances throw him off. He stated that his "lashing out" was not so much directed at Stacey as it was at himself. Bill went on to explain that he believed he should have completed the project he was working on about two weeks ago, but a glitch in the software program had prolonged his efforts. Bill expressed regret that Stacey was afraid of him. Paul asked Bill what he believed an appropriate next step would be. Bill stated that "an apology to Stacey is absolutely appropriate."

Paul agreed that an apology was in order. He then mentioned the company's employee assistance program and suggested the possibility of counseling or even time off. Bill was initially taken aback by these suggestions. He stated that "just because I shouted doesn't mean I've got a mental health problem." Paul maintained an even temperament and explained to Bill that he didn't mean to imply that, that the counseling could be used to help employees get a better handle on how they are perceived by others. Paul explained that it might also be possible that Bill could learn how to ask for help when he needed it. He suggested that if Bill was having trouble with a software program, it might be the program and not Bill that was at fault. Because Bill tended to refuse help, it was impossible for him to know if others were having the same or similar problems. Bill acknowledged that he resisted asking for or receiving assistance because he didn't want to appear weak. Paul assured him that if he chose to use the employee assistance program for counseling, his doing so would be completely confidential. Bill agreed to consider the referral.

Paul closed the meeting by explaining to Bill that the session had been an unofficial counseling session and that it would not affect his performance record. He also stated that he was confident that Bill would apologize to Stacey and that there would be no further incidents of lashing out or using inappropriate language. Paul suggested that he and Bill touch base again in two weeks "just to see how things are going." Bill agreed, and the two men shook hands.

Lesson

Deal with the first sign of violent behavior.

You might be asking yourself, Why all the fuss? All the guy did was swear at a co-worker; what's the big deal? He was a top performer in his department. Who really cares if he occasionally loses his cool? The answer is, Everyone *should* care, and CEC *does*. They understand that one of the best approaches to preventing workplace violence is to nip it in the bud. Besides, it's a lot easier to deal with stage 1 violence than to wait until it escalates to stage 2 or even stage 3.

What did Paul, the HR representative, accomplish in his meeting with Bill? A lot of things. Here are some of them:

- He reminded Bill that the company has a policy prohibiting aggressive language in the workplace.

- He gave Bill some feedback about himself, namely, that he had scared a co-worker by how he responded to her.

- He emphasized that it's okay for Bill to ask for help with a project when he's feeling stressed-out or overwhelmed.

- He also suggested how Bill might take advantage of some company resources (i.e., the employee assistance program) to learn how to avoid such problems in the future.

You may have noticed that Paul never mentioned Bill's past problems with coming in late to work. Was his agenda for the meeting incomplete, or did he simply forget to bring it up? Neither. There was no reason to bring it up since Bill's supervisor indicated that his problems in this area had been resolved long ago. Dredging up this problem from the past would only have made Bill feel picked on and possibly anxious that the company was trying to build a case to fire him. But this problem from the past wasn't relevant to the current issue, and Paul was correct in focusing solely on the issue at hand.

Best Practices Example #2

Paying Attention to Warning Signs

International Vision is one of the largest providers of cable television services in the country. They have offices across the United States. Much of their work involves calling customers on bill-related matters, and some consider the work to be monotonous. There is a very high turnover rate within the organization, and because of this, it's often difficult for workers to get to know each other. International Vision has implemented a workplace violence prevention program that includes a policy prohibiting workplace violence, training for managers, and training for security personnel. International Vision has also established a very good working relationship with local law enforcement departments. On a regular basis, local police officers come into the company to train the in-house security team on issues ranging from theft recovery to defusing irate customers.

Margaret is a 52-year-old customer service representative at International Vision. She is divorced, has no kids, and lives alone. Her co-workers are well aware of the fact that Margaret sees a therapist for the treatment of depression. They know this because Margaret regularly refers to her therapy sessions.

One summer Margaret's therapist went on vacation for a month. The therapist gave Margaret the telephone number of a fellow therapist for Margaret to contact in an emergency.

During the second week of the therapist's vacation, two of Margaret's co-workers noticed that she wasn't completing her work and was spending time staring into space. Not knowing her very well, they decided not to speak to her but rather to their supervisor. After the supervisor received the information from the two co-workers, he decided to call the human resources manager, Laura. The supervisor told Laura what he knew about Margaret and the information received from the two co-workers. Laura decided to ask Margaret to meet with her. First, however, Laura contacted security to inform them that there could be an incident requiring their intervention. Security was put on standby alert. Laura went over to Margaret's workstation and asked her if they could meet privately. Margaret was, of course, caught off guard, and inquired about the reason for the meeting. Laura replied, "You're not in trouble or anything like that. I just want to speak with you about some concerns I have." Margaret agreed and was ushered into a private conference room.

Once they were in the conference room, Laura explained that several of Margaret's co-workers had expressed concern after noting that she seemed depressed. Laura also stated that she would like to assist Margaret if there was any way possible to do so. Margaret said she felt abandoned by her therapist. She said that she had tried to contact the colleague whose name and number her therapist had given her, but found that he too was out of the office. She said that she was "tired of feeling so sad and desperate," and "would probably be better off dead." Laura explained to Margaret that the company would like to place her on paid administrative leave so that she could get appropriate treatment for her depression. Laura asked Margaret if she had a regular doctor in addition to her therapist. Margaret said she did. Laura suggested that together they phone the doctor and try to figure out Margaret's options. After hearing her symptoms and state of mind, the doctor agreed to have Margaret hospitalized and evaluated.

It turned out that Margaret never returned to her position at International Vision, but she did write to Laura to express her gratitude for the time Laura took getting her the help she needed.

Lesson

Everyone is responsible for responding to the warning signs.

Margaret did in fact have a problem: She was battling depression, and when she felt that her therapist had abandoned her, she began to entertain thoughts of suicide. Not only that, but she probably didn't have anyone in her personal life who was close enough to her or who saw her regularly enough to see to it that she got the help she needed. Margaret was probably never at risk to commit an act of violence against anyone other than herself (although once a person reaches that point of not caring, you never know what he or she is capable of). Nevertheless, self-destructive acts are still acts of violence (especially suicide or attempted suicide), and we have a moral obligation as human beings to protect each other from our self-destructive impulses.

The first thing that International Vision did right was that they established an environment in which all employees were aware of the warning signs of violent behavior and felt comfortable speaking up if they noticed any of them. Margaret's co-workers didn't know her well enough to know for a fact that she was considering suicide, but they noticed a decline in her productivity and a change in her personality and/or psychological functioning. And they reported these warning signs to their supervisor.

The other thing that International Vision did right was that they trained their supervisors and managers to respond appropriately when such warning signs were brought to their attention. In particular, Laura, the HR manager, conducted the meeting with Margaret in a sensitive and appropriate manner. As soon as Margaret expressed her suicidal thoughts, Laura's one and only objective was to get Margaret the medical attention she needed so that she wouldn't cause any harm to herself or anyone else.

In this example, the company ended up losing an employee. But they may have saved a life as well. Without a doubt, they helped a troubled employee get the treatment she required before her depression and despondency escalated into violence.

Best Practices Example #3

Correcting Past Oversights and Mistakes

Benson and Benson (B&B) is a large international law firm. They have offices in thirteen U.S. cities and eight international locations. One of the offices is located in a major West Coast city, on the same street as another law firm that experienced a major (and well-publicized) incident of workplace violence several years ago. Several people were actually shot and killed in this infamous incident, and several others were seriously wounded. While no one at B&B was physically hurt or otherwise directly affected by the incident, many staffers were psychologically shaken by such severe violence so close to home. The administrators of the firm took note and decided to implement a proactive violence prevention and intervention program.

While implementing the program, several managers realized that, while they had not identified them as such, there had been a few incidents of workplace violence in the organization in the past. The company's administrators decided to review the previous incidents to determine if they had been handled correctly. While doing so, they discovered that one of the incidents had not been resolved and was still ongoing.

Specifically, there was a male data management staffer named Howard who had regularly asked a female co-worker out socially. The woman had repeatedly explained that she was involved in a relationship and not interested in dating him. However, the male staffer continued to ask her out, and she finally reported this behavior to her supervisor. The supervisor spoke to Howard and explained that his behavior could constitute sexual harassment and must cease immediately. Howard pleaded ignorance and promised that the behavior would end.

While reviewing this and other cases, the company's administrators asked the female employee (1) if the inappropriate behavior had ceased, and (2) if she was satisfied with the way the company had handled the problem. During the interview the woman stated that the "asking out has stopped, but now he just walks up to me and stares." She also stated that she had not bothered to report this latest behavior because, although it made her feel uncomfortable, she "wasn't sure that the staring constituted anything wrong." She reported that she had instead learned to avoid Howard around the office.

B&B reopened the investigation, and in doing so, they discovered three other female employees who described similar experiences with Howard. They also found two male workers who reported feeling uncomfortable around him. One of the men reported that while returning from lunch with a female co-worker (one of the additional three women who also reported being harassed by Howard), Howard threatened him by saying, "If you're smart, you won't flaunt her in my face." The man explained that he took this comment to be "clearly a threat that he did not like seeing me with her."

B&B's administrators recognized that they had a case of sexual harassment on their hands (which is, you will recall, a form of stage 1 violent behavior) and probably an incident of nonsexual workplace violence as well (the threat). They felt helpless, however, to act on the threat since it had occurred *before* the official implementation of their workplace violence policy. However, Howard had been warned (both verbally and in writing) to cease the sexual harassment. Since the behavior had continued (in another form with the same woman, and with additional women as well), they felt perfectly within their rights to terminate him. It was late Thursday afternoon when they came to this decision. So another decision was made: They decided to use Friday and the weekend to develop a plan for terminating Howard and to then meet with him on Monday.

On Friday the building security supervisor was briefed. He was informed that there would be a termination on Monday morning and that security should be present at the meeting. Payroll was contacted and told to issue Howard's final paycheck. Personnel was instructed to collect information regarding Howard's benefits and other payments.

On Monday at 10:00 A.M. Howard was escorted to a conference room. There, he met with his immediate supervisor, human resources, and security. He was informed of the decision to terminate him and why. He was given an opportunity to express himself, though he declined to comment. He was given his final paycheck and told how to continue his medical benefits if he chose. He was also informed of exactly what information would be released if he chose to use Benson and Benson as a reference for future jobs. Finally, he was told that while he was not being terminated because of the threats, the firm was concerned about his threatening behavior nonetheless and had therefore applied for a restraining order. If he was seen attempting to enter the offices, the police would be contacted immediately. They then escorted him off the premises.

After the meeting, all security personnel and receptionists were informed that if they saw Howard attempting to enter the offices, they should call the police immediately, and security should respond in the meantime. Finally, each of the women and the two men who had reported inappropriate interactions with Howard were informed that he was no longer employed with the company. They were also informed that, as a precaution, security would escort them to their cars in the evenings for the next several weeks. Finally, they were given the option of being relocated within the firm, though no one chose this option.

Lesson

If your company doesn't have a violence prevention and intervention program, get one.

Benson and Benson did many things right! First, unaware that they had any violence concerns, they initiated a program to protect their employees and property. Seeing the worst that could happen at another firm, they realized that they were vulnerable. Next, after implementing their new program, they decided to go back and review previous incidents to check the appropriateness and effectiveness of their response. While conducting this review, they determined that at least one incident remained ongoing and still needed to be resolved. This whole scenario demonstrates a willingness on the part of the company's management to acknowledge that they could have and should have done more. Finally, the company took all the appropriate steps in terminating a violent employee to minimize the potential for further violence. The offending male staffer was never seen or heard from again.

chapter **10**

Assessing
Your Organization's
"Violence Quotient"

This chapter consists of eight questionnaires or self-tests that will allow you to assess how well your company is prepared for, prevents, and deals with incidents of workplace violence. These eight tests are listed in the accompanying box on page 166. Take each of the tests; answer the questions as honestly as you can. Add up your total score for each test, then read our analysis of what your score means.

The "scales" we've come up with may be somewhat arbitrary; nevertheless, they should help you to gauge your company's strengths and weaknesses in preventing and responding to incidents of workplace violence. You can consider your company's collective score on these eight self-tests its "violence quotient."

Eight Self-Tests to Determine "Violence Quotient"

1. Workplace violence policy test

2. Crisis management test

3. Training test

4. Security test

5. Legal vulnerability test

6. Employee awareness test

7. Personnel selection test

8. Employee communications test

Use the test results to identify areas in need of improvement, then implement the necessary changes so that your company can be better prepared to deal with the threat and reality of workplace violence.

Workplace Violence Policy Test

This test focuses your attention on your company's workplace violence policy: Is there one, and is it thorough and complete? Remember that most people will do what is expected of them as long as they know what that is. A comprehensive workplace violence policy serves to tell employees what the company expects of them regarding what's appropriate and inappropriate behavior in the workplace. It therefore deters violent behavior. In addition, if you're going to discipline the perpetrators of violent behavior (through suspension or termination, for example), you need a written policy to support such disciplinary action.

This is a true–false test. For each of the following statements, mark T for true and F for false in the spaces provided.

1. ___ Our company has a policy that clearly defines violence and prohibits all acts of violence.

2. ___ Our violence policy describes types of language that are inappropriate as well as acts.

3. ___ All personnel have been made aware of our violence policy through an information campaign.

4. ___ Our violence policy is enforced at all levels within the company.

5. ___ As new information becomes available, we reevaluate our policy.

What Your Score Means

If all five of your answers were true, you're in good shape. If any one of your answers was false, you're not. There's no margin for error in this component of your company's approach to violence. Your company has to have a comprehensive workplace violence policy; your employees have to be made aware of it; and it has to be enforced consistently and updated periodically. If you're falling short in any of these areas, you should make every effort to rectify the situation immediately.

Crisis Management Test

This test focuses your attention on how your company manages violent crises. Every organization needs to designate a team of individuals who will be responsible not only for developing violence prevention policies and response procedures, but also for dealing with violent incidents and individuals as they crop up. This team, which we refer to as the crisis management team, is also responsible for training first-level supervisors, tracking violent incidents within the organization, and serving as the liaison to external law enforcement agencies and the media.

This is a true–false test with three answers possible. For each of the following statements, mark 1, 2, or 3 in the spaces provided, depending on whether the statement is (1) generally not true, (2) sometimes true, or (3) generally true for your organization. Then add the numbers to arrive at a total score for this test.

1. ___ We have a crisis management team (CMT) in our organization.

2. ___ All personnel are aware of the CMT's existence and understand how and when to contact a member of this team.

3. ___ There is an emergency response plan in place that all personnel are familiar with.

4. ___ The CMT tracks violent incidents and is aware of potentially violent employees whose behavior may be escalating.

5. ___ In difficult situations, the CMT provides support and backup to first-level supervisors in confronting violent or potentially violent employees.

6. ___ Members of the CMT have been trained in early threat recognition.

7. ___ Managers and supervisors have also been trained in early threat recognition.

8. ___ Managers and supervisors have been trained in how to document violent incidents.

9. ___ The CMT meets on a regular basis to discuss violent incidents and individuals within the organization.

10. ___ Even when managers and supervisors successfully defuse a potentially violent situation, they still document the incident and forward the report to the CMT.

___ Total

What Your Score Means

26–30   Your organization appears to have gone to great lengths in its proactive stance against violence at work. There seems to be an understanding that a lack of preventive measures often leaves companies and individuals vulnerable to acts of violence.

20–25   Some steps seem to have been taken to develop an action plan to protect employees and the company's assets from acts of violence. It is likely, however, that many of these measures were taken from a minimalist approach. In other words, some of the organizations that have scored in this range have attempted to cut corners in their violence programs. Often their overall philosophy seems to be, "Nothing has happened yet, and even if something does happen, we have *some* measures in place; maybe they'll be enough." Look for ways to expand or improve your preventive efforts.

10–19   We hope that your organization has not had to recover from serious acts of violence. Very often organizations that score in this range have consciously decided that the cost of a violence program is too high given that they have not yet had any major incidents. They have accepted as fact the belief that violence is random and unpredictable. Because of this belief, which is *not* supported by research, they have assumed that any time and effort put into preventive plans would be a waste. But they're taking a big risk. Try sharing some of the data on workplace violence with those administrators in your company who are reluctant to act. Do some research within your own company. Poll employees, supervisors, managers, and others. Ask these individuals if they are aware of incidents of violence that have occurred inside the company. Then share your results with the administrators. Often individuals in administrative positions in a company aren't aware of some of the incidents that others in the company have had to deal with.

Training Test

This test focuses your attention on how well or poorly your organization uses available information. While workplace violence is a growing hazard across the United States, there's no need for panic. Training is the key to reducing the number and severity of violent incidents in your company.

This is a true–false test with three answers possible. For each of the following statements, mark 1, 2, or 3 in the spaces provided, depending on whether the statement is (1) generally not true, (2) sometimes true, or (3) generally true for your organization. Then add the numbers to arrive at a total score for this test.

1. ___ My company understands that violence prevention training is essential in heightening awareness.

2. ___ Not just the members of the crisis management team but all personnel with supervisory duties have been trained to detect and document escalating violence.

3. ___ Each supervisor has been trained to intervene at the first sign of stage 1 or stage 2 violence.

4. ___ The supervisor training includes verbal and physical tactics to defuse violent situations.

5. ___ Managers and supervisors have been trained on how and when to require a fitness-for-duty evaluation for an employee.

6. ___ Supervisory personnel have been trained in how to conduct a safe termination.

7. ___ Supervisory personnel have been taught constructive confrontation techniques.

8. ___ When an employee is promoted to a supervisory position, part of his or her supervisory training focuses on violence prevention.

9. ___ Upper-level managers have received much of the same training as our first-level supervisors, so that there is a common language between the two groups.

10. ___ Our training programs are regularly reviewed and updated so that we can improve the materials presented to our personnel.

___ Total

What Your Score Means

26–30   Your company places appropriate emphasis on violence prevention training for all supervisors and managers. Updating your training from time to time allows you to incorporate new findings and different strategies.

20–25   Your organization offers some training to some personnel. The problem is that those personnel who stand to benefit the most from training probably do not receive as much as they should. It is likely that the members of your crisis management team and other high-level administrators are fairly well trained. However, you must remember that first-level supervisors serve as the eyes and ears for the organization: Train them adequately, and they will be able to serve the company better.

10–19   Your organization doesn't appear to place a high priority on training. You should be aware of the recent increase in the use of terms such as "failure to train" and "failure to train adequately" in lawsuits. Understand that the expense associated with training all supervisory personnel is often offset by a reduction in liability should a violent incident occur. (Training also has the added benefit of increasing morale, which has been associated with increased productivity.)

Security Test

This test focuses your attention on your company's overall organizational security. When we discuss organizational security, people often mistakenly believe that we're talking solely about personnel who wear uniforms and patrol the premises. However, since it is common knowledge that not all organizations have their own security departments, this is a pretty narrow view of security. Organizational security should encompass all practices and procedures that are intended to provide for the safety and protection of all company personnel, property, and assets.

This is a true–false test with three answers possible. For each of the following statements, mark 1, 2, or 3 in the spaces provided, depending on whether the statement is (1) generally not true, (2) sometimes true, or (3) generally true for your organization. Then add the numbers to arrive at a total score for this test.

1. ___ Our organization uses posted signs to discourage customer and client violence.

2. ___ Access to our buildings is limited and/or monitored.

3. ___ We routinely check to make sure that our security measures have not been subverted by our personnel (locked doors propped open, for example).

4. ___ We have provided for the safe handling of valuables (cash, inventory, etc.).

5. ___ Emergency telephone numbers are posted in highly visible and readily available locations.

6. ___ We have established relationships with local law enforcement agencies.

7. ___ When an individual is no longer employed by our company, he or she no longer has access to our organization (keys, badges, and I.D. are recovered, for example).

8. ___ Our organization seeks restraining orders against individuals (former employees, customers, and/or vendors) who present a threat to the safety and security of our personnel or property.

9. ___ All members of this company have been informed that they are to report suspicious, violent, and/or bizarre behavior to security (or if no security department exists, then to some other designated department).

10. ___ All company personnel understand the three responsibilities a person has when encountering stage 3 violence.

___ Total

What Your Score Means

26–30   Your company clearly takes its organizational security seriously. With or without a security department, the administrators understand that safety is everyone's responsibility. We hope that you and your organization will never have to respond to a violent emergency. However, if you ever do, your company is well prepared to deal with it.

20–25   Your company has taken some steps to provide for the safety of company personnel and assets. There are some gaps and lapses, however. One of the most significant findings in a recent security survey was that although many companies have adequate security measures in place, these are often subverted by people who have become complacent. A card-key entry system is useless if personnel prop the door open when they go out for a smoke. Likewise, having security guards and receptionists monitor people entering and exiting the building serves no purpose if at lunchtime most employees exit through a fire door because it is closer to the parking lot. Be sure that your organization does spot security checks to determine how consistently your security measures are actually used or followed. Develop relationships with members of local law enforcement agencies. Often police departments have a community relations division that will send an officer out to your company's premises to perform a security evaluation for you. This is often a free service and is of great value in improving the security of your organization.

10–19   Didn't anyone ever tell you that an ounce of prevention is worth a pound of cure? Granted, no measure of security completely eliminates the possibility of violence. However, companies that implement a security program lessen their odds of having to attempt to recover after a major violent incident. Often, organizations that score in this range are denying the possibility of violence or simply throwing their corporate arms in the air in a symbol of helplessness. If your company fits that description, encourage the administrators in your organization to develop security procedures to help protect the company's assets *and* its employees. In the meantime, make sure that you yourself have a personal security plan and know how you would respond to a violent incident.

Legal Vulnerability Test

This test focuses your attention on your company's legal vulnerability with regard to violence-related lawsuits. Organizations generally fall into two major categories with respect to workplace violence and liability: Either they implement a program exclusively designed to reduce liability, or they fail to address liability altogether. Both approaches leave the company and its employees unprotected.

The organization that makes a feeble attempt to discourage violence with a poorly conceived policy or program usually finds that it has neither protected its employees nor reduced its liability. Unfortunately, the incidence of workplace violence has been on the rise—and seems to be continuing to increase. Because of this trend, there is more helpful research and support on the topic available now than ever before. This research often includes what measures have been shown to reduce the incidence of violence. Just as important, however, the research often indicates which measures seem to have had no impact. With all the literature out there, it is unlikely that anyone in a position to judge would be fooled into thinking that the company with a poorly conceived policy or program really made a reasonable attempt to prevent workplace violence and protect its personnel.

The organization that implements a program of violence prevention and intervention *without* addressing personal liability is doing a disservice to its employees. When a program is implemented, each supervisor and manager must be told that there have been precedent cases in which managers who failed to act appropriately have been held (by the courts) partially responsible for the consequences of their negligence. When a manager who has been trained by his or her employer to observe, document, and intervene in response to certain behaviors *fails* to do so, that individual then shares with the parent organization liability for the results of the inappropriate acts. In other words, by virtue of having received training, managers assume some of the responsibility for keeping the workplace safe.

Having a violence prevention and intervention program in place serves to protect the people and assets that form your company. It also serves to provide a legally defensible position should a violent incident occur. There are some administrators who gamble that nothing will ever happen in their organization; but few would argue with the premise that if there is an incident of actual physical violence, there will also be a lawsuit. The United States is the most litigious nation in the world. We have more attorneys per capita than any other country. If you accept the documented statistic stated in the April 1995 issue, "Be a Manager, Go to Jail," from the Scripps Center International Newsletter, Volume 2, that the incidence of workplace violence is going up about 6 percent a year, then you must also acknowledge that your organization will have to deal with an incident one of these days. There will also likely be a lawsuit. How well is your company prepared to defend its practices?

This is a true–false test with three answers possible. For each of the following statements, mark 1, 2, or 3 in the spaces provided, depending on whether the statement is (1) generally not true, (2) sometimes true, or (3) generally true for your organization. Then add the numbers to arrive at a total score for this test.

1. ___ Our company routinely includes corporate counsel in discussions about our violence policy.

2. ___ Our corporate counsel keeps him- or herself informed and up to date on workplace violence issues.

3. ___ Our violence policy and program is in line with OSHA guidelines for a safe, secure, and hostile-free workplace.

4. ___ A member of our legal department serves on our crisis management team.

5. ___ We keep on file a record of the violence prevention training our employees have received.

6. ___ Each new hire signs our policy on workplace violence, indicating that he or she understands it and will act within it. We keep a record of this contract.

7. ___ The potential consequences of breaking the workplace violence policy are spelled out in every employment contract.

8. ___ When our legal counsel makes a recommendation in the areas of safety and security, we follow it.

9. ___ When our company considers severe disciplinary actions (involuntary leave, suspension, or termination, for example), our legal counsel reviews the plan to insure that it is in line with our stated policies.

10. ___ We are consistent in the application of our workplace violence policy.

11. ___ Our managers and supervisors understand their duty to report and document violent behavior, and how this influences their personal liability.

12. ___ Our managers and supervisors understand that they are required to investigate certain behaviors whether or not a complaint is filed.

13. ___ Upper management understands that they assume some liability whether or not they were even aware of an incident of violence.

14. ___ Our managers and supervisors understand that they sometimes assume as much liability, if not more, when they don't get involved as when they do.

15. ___ Our company administrators have made it clear to all personnel that they have implemented a workplace violence program to prevent injuries, save lives, and decrease liability.

___ Total

What Your Score Means

40–45   Your organization seems to be well aware of the legal risks, and appears to have taken appropriate steps to mitigate those risks. Having your legal counsel participate in company decisions regarding violence policies and programs is a plus, and will likely add support to any legal defense the company may have to mount in the future.

30–39   Your company probably solicits the opinion of legal advisors but doesn't follow that advice on a consistent basis. Advise those in your organization to be careful. Knowing the right thing to do and not doing it can lead to greater liability than being ignorant. If you are in a management or supervisory role, be sure to document all inappropriate behaviors that come to your attention. Make sure that you send these reports to others in your company (your supervisor, human resources, security, etc.). Be certain that you are never caught in a scenario in which an incident has occurred, you knew about it, but you neglected to make others aware of the problem.

15–29   Your organization is vulnerable to violence-related lawsuits. If you are a supervisor or manager, there are two things you should do: (1) At every opportunity, encourage the administrators in your company to seek out the counsel of legal experts. When there is a situation that involves potential liability, make sure you are the one who asks, "Have we run this by legal yet?" Even if your organization *doesn't* have a legal department or internal counsel, encourage the administration to seek outside legal advice *before* a problem arises. (2) Always document incidents that you perceive to be indicative of potential violence. Intervene (based on our recommendations in chapter 7) when appropriate. Be sure to submit your written report of the incident up the chain of command. Consider keeping a journal record of violent incidents and your responses to them. Include in this journal the dates and times of incidents, outcomes, and most important, to whom you forwarded your documentation. This may perhaps serve you well personally until your organization recognizes and acts on its need to protect itself.

Employee Awareness Test

This test focuses your attention on how well your organization keeps its personnel informed—both about its violence policy and about other matters that may be important to them. Having a policy against violence that no one is aware of until it has been breached doesn't serve to deter anyone. In addition, while no one *causes* another person to be violent, there are certain factors that can be said to *allow* a violent person to act out in an escalating manner. These factors are called triggering events. For example, imagine the stress placed on workers who know about a pending layoff for nine months but don't know if they are slated to be cut. They aren't allowed to plan and project ahead in their lives. They often begin to feel that they are pawns in a company chess game, and have no particular value to the organization. It should surprise no one that their loyalty and dedication to the organization can sometimes diminish, and that they may act inappropriately as a result.

This is a true–false test with three answers possible. For each of the following statements, mark 1, 2, or 3 in the spaces provided, depending on whether the statement is (1) generally not true, (2) sometimes true, or (3) generally true for your organization. Then add the numbers to arrive at a total score for this test.

1. ___ Our personnel are aware of our workplace violence policy.

2. ___ Our personnel have been informed of emergency response procedures.

3. ___ Our personnel know whom to contact if they are ever feeling threatened or endangered in any way on the job.

4. ___ Our employees know that all violent threats are taken seriously and will be investigated.

5. ___ Our employees understand that violence from customers will not be tolerated.

6. ___ While financial assets are obviously important, our employees know that their safety is more important to the organization.

7. ___ Our personnel are familiar with the warning signs of potential violence.

8. ___ Our employees believe that investigations into inappropriate behavior are handled discreetly, and they therefore feel free to report such incidents.

9. ___ When there is any kind of violent behavior in this organization, our employees perceive that their well-being is the first concern of administrators.

10. ___ When the company is anticipating job cuts, layoffs, or other major changes that affect employees, the administration keeps them informed and up to date so that they can make accommodations in their lives.

___ Total

What Your Score Means

26–30   Your company values the people who make it work, and they know it. They are kept informed and up to date, on violence-related policies and attitudes especially. There is likely a great sense of loyalty among your employees, with most of them feeling supported. An employee who witnessed another individual acting out would probably feel comfortable reporting the incident. Be sure to continue to inform your employees as the company's goals and directives change, and they will probably continue to inform you of trouble areas.

20–25   The good news is that your organization has taken some steps toward creating an atmosphere of openness. There are also indications that the administrators have acknowledged that workplace violence exists. The bad news is that there seem to be some inconsistencies in how these issues are dealt with. There are probably times when incidents are not taken seriously and/or not handled discreetly. This inconsistency can lead to frustration on the part of your personnel. It could also lead to occasions when reportable incidents are not reported, thereby taking away the possibility of intervening before it is too late. Encourage the administrators in your organization to be more precise in the development, interpretation, and implementation of violence policies. Make sure that some of your employees and employee representatives participate in this process. This serves two purposes: (1) It sends feedback up the chain of command about what occurs on a regular basis, and (2) it sends the message to employees that the company is attempting to make people a priority.

10–19   Your employees probably do *not* come forward to keep the administration informed of problems or potential problems. This may result from the fact that the administration doesn't seem to keep employees informed. It appears that much of what goes on in your organization happens without much communication or exchange of information. Yet this environment can be a breeding ground for the escalation of inappropriate behavior.

Consider doing employee surveys. These can be quite simple. One company used paycheck envelopes to distribute brief questionnaires to their employees. They simply inserted a ten-question survey into the envelopes and distributed them as usual on payday. The survey was anonymous, but there was a line where the employee could put his or her name and number if the employee agreed to be interviewed. The survey results helped the company begin implementation of a safety and security program.

Personnel Selection Test

This test focuses your attention on how well your company screens prospective employees in an effort to hire only the most appropriate candidates. When a company hires a new employee, the expectation is that that individual will contribute to the company's business efforts while conducting him- or herself in a manner consistent with the company's philosophy. As we all know, there are times when these expectations aren't met and the new hire doesn't work out. This can happen even when the company has thoroughly screened the applicant before hiring him or her. More often, though, when a new hire doesn't work out, the screening of that applicant was cursory or incomplete.

This is a true–false test with three answers possible. For each of the following statements, mark 1, 2, or 3 in the spaces provided, depending on whether the statement is (1) generally not true, (2) sometimes true, or (3) generally true for your organization. Then add the numbers to arrive at a total score for this test.

1. ___ My company checks all references of prospective employees.

2. ___ An applicant is immediately rejected if we determine that he or she lied on his or her résumé or application.

3. ___ Applicants must supply both personal and professional references.

4. ___ Prospective employees are given accurate information about performance requirements and possibilities for advancement *before* they are hired.

5. ___ New hires are required to read and sign our workplace violence policy.

6. ___ One of the steps in our hiring process is an interview during which we explore inconsistencies between what the applicant says and his or her written résumé and application.

7. ___ When there are questions or concerns about a person's work history, we thoroughly explore those concerns before hiring that person.

8. ___ Our recruiters place higher emphasis on the honesty and integrity of applicants than on any other quality.

9. ___ From time to time our recruiters poll supervisors to see how new hires are doing in the company. This feedback helps improve our hiring process.

10. ___ When an individual is hired, we make sure that part of his or her initial training focuses on conflict resolution.

___ Total

What Your Score Means

26–30   Your company seems to understand that your new hires are your raw materials: Start with the best raw materials, and you're closer to the desired end result. Start with less-than-desirable raw materials, and your end product can suffer. Your organization seems to take the screening of new applicants seriously. There may, however, be some areas in which you could improve your hiring process. Maybe you need to be more consistent in the feedback loop, so that recruiters can better understand how and why their choices succeeded or failed. With this information, they can tweak their approach for even better future results.

20–25   Your company seems to have recognized the need for stringent screening measures, but seems to apply them only sometimes. Before positions are filled, speak to managers and supervisors in the department in which there is an opening. Find out why and how people are successful in those departments. Don't just rely on old, sometimes outdated job descriptions. Be sure to speak to employees who hold similar positions to the one being filled: They can offer valuable assistance in choosing a good fit. Remember that all new hires have the potential to be in the company for a very long time. If there are problems with the applicant before the hire, they are likely to get worse over time.

10–19   Your company's perspective on selecting personnel may be "You need a job? We have work." Consider, however, that hiring someone is similar in many respects to getting married: Many marriages fail in part because one or both parties entered into the union believing that they could change the undesirable qualities in their mate. Likewise, many employer-employee relationships don't work in part because the employer believed that the negative habits or qualities of the applicant could be trained away. Overwhelmingly, organizations find that the most violence-prone individuals in their companies have long histories of troubled employment. Therefore, it makes a lot of sense to put more time, energy, and resources into screening and selecting applicants carefully.

Employee Communications Test

This test focuses your attention on the need for organizations to be honest with not only job seekers but also their current employees. There is a tendency in corporations to encourage, often unwittingly, unrealistic expectations. For example, allowing part-time and temporary employees to falsely believe that it is only a matter of time before they'll be hired on a full-time and/or permanent basis. Or allowing an individual to continue applying for advancement even though it is clear that he or she isn't ready for, and won't get, the promotion. Another common practice is the failure to give honest feedback so that the employee can improve in areas where he or she is weak or set more attainable goals.

Most often these acts of dishonesty are attempts to spare feelings. Sometimes they're the result of managers not feeling comfortable giving feedback that might be perceived as negative. Sometimes, too, there's a fear of losing employees if they know they are unlikely to ever be promoted. However, these attitudes and beliefs are all faulty. For this type of thinking doesn't acknowledge that some people are content in nonsupervisory positions, some people are satisfied with part-time and/or temporary work, and we all need to know if we're likely to be laid off soon or unlikely to receive a promotion we seek. Allowing an employee to have false expectations sets that individual up for a big disappointment—maybe even feeling that he or she has been betrayed or at least treated unfairly by the organization. And those are feelings that may lead to violent behavior.

This is a true–false test with three answers possible. For each of the following statements, mark 1, 2, or 3 in the spaces provided, depending on whether the statement is (1) generally not true, (2) sometimes true, or (3) generally true for your organization. Then add the numbers to arrive at a total score for this test.

1. ___ When we are considering a new candidate for hire, that person is given accurate information about the possibilities for future advancement in the organization.

2. ___ When a person is hired for part-time or temporary work, that person is accurately informed of the realistic possibility that the position will evolve into full-time and/or permanent work.

3. ___ Possible layoffs are discussed openly in our organization.

4. ___ When layoffs are on the horizon, we encourage our employees to begin to consider their options, while still requiring 100 percent effort from them at work.

5. ___ Promotions are fair, and the promotion process is well understood.

6. ___ Before we promote anyone to a supervisory position, our promotional review process includes evaluating how well that individual relates to his or her peers.

7. ___ We recognize that not everyone can be (or even wants to be) a supervisor or manager. Therefore, we have developed other means to acknowledge and reward outstanding performance among our employees.

8. ___ We give honest feedback to those employees who are seeking advancement. Therefore, while we allow people to apply for any position they choose, we encourage our employees to develop reasonable expectations.

9. ___ Part-time and temporary employees are treated with the same dignity and respect as others in our organization.

10. ___ Our grievance process is well publicized within our company.

___ Total

What Your Score Means

26–30   Your organization seems to recognize the necessity of honest employee communications. It also appears that your company understands that people are different and have different needs and desires regarding their employment status and moving up the corporate ladder.

20–25   There are probably those in your organization who understand the significance of helping others establish realistic expectations. There are also probably those who find it difficult to openly discuss anything that might be perceived as negative. The need for a fair and honest promotional process is probably understood but sometimes ignored by decision makers in your company.

10–19   The prevailing philosophy in your organization might be summarized as, "Tell people only what they need to know at the time." This approach might placate your staff for a while, but eventually they will become cynical. Also, there may be a tendency in your company to hire individuals under false pretenses. If that's the case, be careful! While there is no clear correlation between part-time or temporary employment and violence, nor between status in the hierarchy of an organization and violence, there *is* a correlation between unmet expectations and violence. Encourage honest and open discussion and feedback in your company. This will keep your employees from feeling kept in the dark or treated unfairly, and will allow them to consider other options in a positive, constructive manner if their needs and desires are not being met in their current situation.

Summary of the Steps for Instituting a Program

The incidence of workplace violence is on the rise; as cited on page 175, some estimates suggest that it increases by 6 percent a year. This trend is a sad comment on the state of American society, but it need not spell doom for your company. Just as home owners and car owners take measures to protect their families and property (locking doors and windows, installing alarm systems, and buying insurance policies), the administrators of companies and organizations can and should take measures to reduce the impact of violence at work. In particular, there are four essential steps we recommend you take to institute a workplace violence prevention and intervention program in your organization:

1. *Develop a workplace violence policy.* This is the first and most basic step; everything else will follow from this. And before

you get intimidated by the thought of creating a brand-new policy, consider that your workplace violence policy can often be adapted from your sexual harassment policy (which we hope you already have): The basic objective of both is to prohibit any behavior that would tend to create a hostile work environment. (You can also adapt a workplace violence policy from the sample policy we included in chapter 5.)

2. *Select and train a crisis management team.* The crisis management team should consist of six to ten managers from a variety of disciplines within the organization (human resources, security, legal affairs, etc.). They will become the company's in-house experts on violence-related policies and response procedures—responsible not only for developing those policies and procedures but also for training first-level supervisors, tracking violent incidents and individuals, and serving as the liaison to law enforcement agencies and the media in cases of severe violence. Each member of the team should be assigned a specific role and responsibilities. (Once the company's violence program has been implemented, the increased workload that these responsibilities entail should be minimal.)

3. *Train first-level supervisors and managers.* First-level supervisors and managers are the eyes and ears of the company: They are usually the first to detect or be aware of a potential problem. Given the importance of early intervention in minimizing and reducing the effects of workplace violence, first-level supervisors and managers must be given as much information and training as possible, to help them to recognize the warning signs of violent behavior and intervene appropriately to ward it off or nip it in the bud.

4. *Establish an employee awareness program.* Once a workplace violence policy and a crisis management team are in place, and first-level supervisors and managers have been trained to recognize the warning signs of violent behavior and intervene appropriately, the final step in implementing an effective workplace violence prevention and intervention program is to make sure that all employees know about all of this. Disseminate your policy; hold companywide meetings to present and discuss it. All employees need to know (1) what is considered violent behavior, (2) how to report incidents of such behavior, and (3) what the consequences will be for exhibiting such behavior. Have employees sign the policy to indicate that they've read it, understand it, and agree to abide by it.

appendix B

Resources

You can implement many of the recommendations offered in this book using your own in-house resources. In addition, there are many individuals and organizations available to provide assistance to your company, on a consultancy basis, in developing and strengthening a workplace violence prevention and intervention program. A number of such consulting organizations are listed below.

In seeking assistance from such consultants, be sure to do your homework. Ask if the consultant has provided services to other companies in your industry. Ask for references that you can contact. In other words, be as thorough in your screening of a security consultant as you would be in hiring a new applicant or choosing a vendor for an important contract.

Academy Group, Inc.   (703) 330-0697
9304 Peabody Street
Manassas, VA 22110

Crisis Management Group   (617) 969-7600
381 Elliot Street, Suite 180L
Newton Upper Falls, MA 02164

Issac Ray Center, Inc.   (312) 829-8021
1725 West Harrison Street, Suite 110
Chicago, IL 60612

National Assessment Services   (415) 512-1293
333 Market Street, Suite 3110
San Francisco, CA 94105

National Safe Workplace Institute   (704) 841-1175
2400 Crown Point Drive, Suite 100
Charlotte, NC 28227

Scientech, Inc.   (301) 468-6425
11140 Rockville Pike, Suite 500
Rockville, MD 20852

Scripps Center International   (619) 566-3472
10085 Carroll Canyon Road, Suite 240
San Diego, CA 92131

About the Author

Dennis A. Davis is a nationally recognized expert in the field of violence prevention and intervention and holds a Ph.D. in psychology. In addition to this book, Dr. Davis has published numerous articles on workplace violence and offers consulting services to private corporations, government agencies, and educational institutions to help them establish and maintain violence-free environments.

In his consulting work, Dr. Davis has assembled a team of expert associates from a variety of disciplines who work with him to meet the particular needs of individual clients. These associates include clinical psychologists, attorneys, and human resources professionals as well as security specialists.

Dr. Davis and his associates can help you with the following specific tasks:

- Training your personnel how to manage irate (and potentially violent) customers

- Training your personnel how to better deal with cultural diversity

- Training your personnel how to prevent and respond to sexual harassment

- Training your personnel how to resolve conflicts more effectively

- Developing and implementing workplace violence prevention and intervention programs

- Developing and implementing workplace violence policies and response procedures

- Selecting and training a crisis management team

- Counseling affected individuals after a critical incident has occurred to help them cope better with the trauma

- Determining your organization's "violence quotient"

If you have any questions or comments on the guidelines offered in this book, or would like further information about Dr. Davis's consulting services, you can contact him through ther publisher.

Index